Hidden S

Attract Everything You Want

Hidden Secrets
Attract Everything You Want

Carl Nagel

First edition
Published in Great Britain
By Mirage Publishing 2009

First published in paperback 2009

A CIP catalogue record for this book
is available from the British Library.

ISBN: 978-1-902578-42-2

Mirage Publishing
PO Box 161
Gateshead
NE8 1WY
Great Britain

Printed and bound in Great Britain by

Book Printing UK
Remus House, Coltsfoot Drive, Woodston, Peterborough, PE2 9JX

Papers used in the production of this book are recycled,
thus reducing environmental depletion.

To all who dream of changing their lives

Contents

Introduction

Some of my earliest childhood memories are of Sunday afternoon Ouija board sessions with family members, the kitchen table acting as a makeshift talking board. A lot of what came through was, on reflection, gibberish. Of course it was gibberish, 90% of spirits contacted in this manner are mischievous by nature and delight in leading us astray. It takes patience to make sense of what comes through, to sift the grains of gold from the sands of nonsense.

Spirits, of whom there are millions, inhabit the Invisible World around us. Through the pages of this book you will experience first-hand this phantasmagorical world of faceless entities, restless ghosts, venomous supernatural creatures, fallen angels, alien visitors, disembodied entities and things that go bump in the night.

Here, too, are the working tools of Magic, and how to use them to make strange and wonderful things happen in your life. Within these pages you will discover the secrets of how to use Spells and Rituals to attract money, win love, dispel evil, and much more.

Yes, you will find mysteries in these pages. The strange creatures from time and space described here do exist. But you will also find a practical way of getting the things you seek. No long philosophical meanderings; just simple, straightforward instructions that will help you to improve your quality of life.

I am going to teach you what I know works. I have taught the secrets of how to cast Spells and work Rituals to scores of people in person, by mail, over the phone and even over the Internet with equal success.

I have taken those very same Spells and Rituals that have proved so successful for others and included them in this book. You can use them yourself to make things easier.

In this unusual book, you're going to see how to 'awaken' the magic power of witchcraft. In simple, plain language you'll discover what witchcraft really is, how you can master it and how you can use it in lots of different ways for such things as attracting a steady flow of cash, winning perfect love, invoking the secret forces of nature, and much more.

Nothing is held back, nothing is concealed - it's all placed right in your hands, ready to be used for such things as arousing passion in another, making money appear as if from out of thin air, or attracting the opposite sex.

In reading these words you will learn many ancient secrets of the occult. No matter whether you believe me or not, the magic behind these words will awaken racial memories of a time long ago when this secret knowledge was free to every man and woman who sought it.

You Can Be a Witch

You have a Power within you that can be woken. It is the same Power that you can use to work any Magic you want. Many witches work alone and with just as good results using the Magic Power of witchcraft as if they were working with a group. Using this magical power is simplicity itself.

In Chapter 3 you will learn a simple Ritual that will summon the magical energy within you. When this Ritual has been completed, you will have made a very definite contact with the Magic Power of witchcraft.

The old Grimoires, hand-written books of magic, were most specific in what they said about the art and practice of magic. Dark forests, secluded caves, abandoned ruins, or upon the seashore beneath a full moon were considered as ideal places to work Magic. You do not have to do anything so elaborate. Some space and a few minutes of your time each day is all that is required for you to work Magic.

Secrets of Money Magic

This aspect of the Occult is one of the most popular. In Chapter 4 you are going to see how you can use the Magic Power of Spells to bring money.

These Spells have proven extremely successful in bringing moderate amounts of money to meet financial needs. The effects of these Money Spells may not be as dramatic as winning a lottery, but things will become generally better for you as needs are met and existing assets are increased.

Here, too, is the secret of how to cast Spells that really work. A Spell, simply defined, is a set of words spoken that are believed to exert a magical effect on a situation that the person casting the spell seeks to change. The casting of Spells is based upon the ancient belief that to speak a desire is to cause the desire to be fulfilled.

Secrets of Sex Magic

Have you ever seen a beautiful woman in the company of a real nerd, and wondered how he got so lucky?

Maybe it was Sex Magic. In the eternal story of men chasing women, and vice versa, it should always be remembered that Witchcraft and Sex Magic have seduced more members of the opposite sex than any amount of good looks, intelligence or position.

Sex Magic can influence and attract the opposite sex like nothing else can. It can compel a girl to introduce herself to a man in whom she had no previous interest. Sex Magic as it is practised today is revealed in Chapter 8.

Secrets of the Cabala

The saints, sages and wise men of a time long ago discovered that certain Cabalistic Rites and Ceremonies created powerful mystic vibrations that sought similar vibrations within the depths of the Invisible World, to become one pulsating force of Mystic Power. The physical manifestation of this Power was called Magic.

You will soon be working real Magic with the same Power experienced by these wizards of the ages. The Power of the Spheres is waiting for you to put it into dynamic action to transform your life into whatever you want it to be.

Chapter 5 tells you exactly how to use the magical power of the Cabala to increase your money supply.

Secrets of Genuine Ancient Magic

An essential part of the Occult Arts is the conjuring of Spirits. This is something that occultists have been doing for centuries, and now you can join their ranks.

There are ancient occult forces for good or evil. To receive the help these forces can give, it is necessary to make contact.

The secret of conjuring powerful Ancient Spirits is disclosed in Chapter 9. There you'll see how you can cast fast-acting Spells to bring you what you seek and magically smooth your path through life.

Here, too, you will discover how to make a Magic Money Jar that fills with money whenever you need it.

The Land Unknown

The meaning of signs and omens are revealed in Chapter 6, and a most unusual psychic technique that will enable you to actually 'see' the invisible world around you. What will you see in this way? That I leave you to find out, but it will be unlike anything you have ever seen or experienced before. Here, too, is the secret of UFO Dreaming, and how one may make contact with alien minds.

The Sound of Silence

There is a silent voice that speaks to us from the Inner Planes of the Invisible World. Through the use of dice you can quickly learn how to 'hear' this silent voice to foretell future events with amazing accuracy. The inhabitants of the Invisible World know the future and are ready to share its secrets with you.

You Can Work Magic

There should be no doubt in your mind that the amazing secrets of the Invisible World revealed to you within this book are going to work for you. Why? Because I am only going to teach you what I know works.

Many people have said that I am 'lucky'. And why not? I am lucky and I am happy - and I am going to prove that you too can enjoy happiness and good fortune.

One very practical application of occult power is in the area of increased prosperity.

These amazing secrets of the Invisible World can bring you good fortune beyond your wildest dreams. I should know. I have used them to win over AU$10,000 in lotteries and contests – and you can do the same.

Carl Nagel

Chapter 1

THE UNINVITED

I first became involved with the occult arts as such through the now defunct Psychic Research Society of Australia. Thinking it involved actual research, you can imagine my dismay when I found that it seemed to have been taken over completely by little old ladies with blue rinses trying to make contact with a loved one recently departed, i.e. Spiritualism!

All was not lost however; I remember a day in December 1978 when something uninvited came to visit.

I had become a member of the Society a mere four weeks earlier to study the mysteries of the soul and the universe, only to find the subject bewildering and full of apparent contradictions.

The weekly meetings were confined to exercises in ESP and lectures on the limitless virtues of spiritualism which Ivan, the psychic who ran the class, believed were the main interests to the sitters.

I had joined the organisation in the hope of gaining an insight into the benefits, material and spiritual, that could be quickly gained by the study and application of occultism and one's own higher instincts, only to find the weekly classes both repetitive and dull.

The Grey Man

We had gathered together in the small room that served as a meeting place, discussing things beyond the physical touch, of seeing the future with our unseeing eyes, when a ghostly figure walked right through a closed door into the room where we were seated. It shuffled across the room towards a somewhat sinister-looking man and slowly raised its arm and pointed at him. Then abruptly it was gone.

There was something special and very familiar about the mysterious entity and its actions. But from the view of the people who were with me that day, something very unusual (unusual, that is, for them) had happened. They had never before been confronted in the middle of the afternoon by a tall grey entity of apparently supernatural origin.

They knew nothing about it or the reasons for its presence so they were forced to speculate. Why would a ghostlike apparition suddenly appear in their midst?

The Society was like a second home to me in those days. I had a few friends there. One of them, Ralph, a government employee with an interest in paranormal phenomena, was with me that day. He had been given the task of running the class whilst Ivan was away on vacation, and as we talked on into the late afternoon it was difficult to know if we really had seen something in the room.

We had to consider that it could have been a shadow cast by something going past the window.

I had been sitting facing the window with my eyes closed when the entity came and stood in front of me, blocking out the sunlight shining in through the window. I had an interesting emotional reaction (interesting, that is, to me) to this event.

I felt a strange sensation. Something indefinite, haunting. Something half-forgotten, a far away memory returning again.

When I was six or seven years old, one bright sunny day, I was playing in the backyard of the family home when I happened to look up and saw a tall, grey-coloured entity standing over me.

It made no sound and had no eyes, ears, nose, mouth, or anything like that. It was just like a solid grey form.

I screamed aloud and shouted for my parents, but the entity vanished before anyone else had time to see it.

I would prefer to believe that my presence in the class that December did not cause the strange entity to appear. I certainly had no inclination of what was to come. The Society no longer exists now. But I still remember. I remember the Grey Man, as I have come to call him, and the effect his brief presence had upon the people gathered in the small room that fateful day.

After leaving the society, I read as many books as I could on the subject of mind power, magic, witchcraft and the occult. I learnt a lot from those books on the basics of how Rituals are formed and the format for applying one's mental abilities. However, they were not of the type you would normally associate with magical practice.

I tried to read Aleister Crowley's *Magick in Theory and Practice,* but it was written in such a convoluted manner that it was, to me, almost like trying to read Latin without ever having learned the language. As a consequence, I began forming my own Spells and Rituals based on occult tradition.

The Unseen World

The Grey Man was, I believe, one of the many mysterious entities that populate an invisible sphere of existence, which duplicates the physical world in which we live.

To experience this unseen world you must first rid yourself of old thought patterns and open your mind to other realities beyond this sphere. Everything radiates energy. Pick an object in your home that you look at every day, which you believe to be almost alive.

Now begin to believe it *is* alive!

It is very simple to do this and when it appears to blink (if the object is a figurine) or move, transformation will take place like a light being switched on inside your mind. Once this happens, expect various remarkable phenomena to occur. Shadows will come alive, flowers will speak, and the invisible will become visible.

The psychic formula which I have just described was given to me by a disembodied entity, during the world's strangest telephone conversation with a psychic medium, on the evening of 23 April 1993.

The inhabitants of the unseen world have made repeated attempts to explain the occult mysteries in terms that we might understand.

On 4 February 1994, an entity calling itself 'Va' passed this message along to me:

'The energies of which we speak are natural, in that they are of the Earth. You have only to close your eyes and speak their name for them to come to you, and manifest their powers in your life. We are here to guide you onto the path of enlightenment for others who will come to you in your life.

'There are many ways to obtain the insight that you seek through us, but only one true path for each. This is the wisdom of the ages come to pass. We have neither the need nor the desire for names, such is a human failing. Man has given us names.

'The astral realm around you exists to be explored through thought. The astral body, of which much has been written, exists as the storehouse of the eternal soul as man describes it. We know it as energy given substance. The astral body is not designed to journey out of the host body. Only at death does this take place, so that its individual energies can merge with the collective whole. It is one's awareness, one's thoughts that can enter the astral realms around you.'

The astral body is an exact invisible duplicate of the physical body. Occult tradition states that it regularly leaves the sleeping body during sleep, although there is no clear memory of this when you wake. Once you are out of body you are, in effect, an invisible spirit entity and the concept of reality no longer has meaning.

Anyone with a basic understanding of occult laws will know that many outrageous claims have been made regarding the alleged advantages to be gained from the conscious projection of the astral body from its physical counterpart: traveling great distances in an instant, visits to other planets, witnessing the secret activities of others, and so forth.

The astral world around us is mysterious, awesome and sometimes frightening.

Behind Evil Eyes

There is an apartment block on a tree-lined suburban street which once harboured a very strange ghost within its walls. You won't find this particular member of the restless dead listed in any catalogue of ghosts, even though its psychic influence was felt by several people during the autumn of 1982. There were never any reports of haunting there until after a young man moved into the apartment in question.

For many years he had spent all his spare time studying books of arcane lore; all of them centred around the ability to tune-in to the invisible world of spirits and psychic phenomena, and many of those books were read in the apartment in suburbia. Which brings us to the question, why would a phantom suddenly appear in a modern apartment? Could it have been some kind of reaction to the young man's presence, and to the nature of his studies?

I was that young man, and for me it began with an unwelcome visitor from the beyond.

I had been relaxing in the living room, watching television before going to bed, when a gnawing sense of evil suddenly overwhelmed me. I had the sensation that something *unseen* had entered the room. I tried to banish it from my mind and concentrate on the TV programme, a movie about white-slavery in

Tangiers, but the chill malevolence remained.

I took a deep breath and tried to remain calm. Then, without warning, the air seemed to become charged with electricity. A weird prickling sensation spread over my body. This is it, I thought. But the disturbing manifestation ceased as abruptly as it had began.

I was both perplexed and relieved. My uninvited guest had slipped silently away into the night - a transient phantom that had disappeared before I could understand it. It was almost midnight and the evening's events had left me feeling weak. I resolved to get a good night's sleep and tackle the problem of what it had all meant in the morning.

And then the nightmare began.

I gently drifted up and out of my sleeping body. Before I had a chance to realise what was happening, I saw it. In the darkness, at the far end of the hallway, something was taking form.

Silhouetted against the moonlit living room beyond, a macabre event was taking place.

There it was, as clear as crystal, out of nowhere the ghost of a little girl had come to visit. She stared at me. Her eyes were dark pits of implacable hatred.

The image of those evil eyes burned deep into my memory, never to be forgotten. The malevolent spirit began to move silently towards me. My chest tightened and my heart began to pound as a primeval fear from deep within the human psyche overwhelmed me.

I watched as the spirit moved ever closer. I tried to scream but could not. I felt the icy touch of pure evil upon me.

I awoke bathed in sweat.

A few days later I had another bad dream in which I sat before a large, ornate mirror looking at my reflection in the glass. The image suddenly changed into a dark simulacrum. It sat there, an evil grin upon its face, mocking me. And from its left hand there came forth a giant vampire bat.

Then suddenly there was loud knocking on the bedroom door. I sat up in bed, trembling. The knocking ceased. I went to the door, put my hand on the knob and hesitantly opened it.

The hall was empty.

I closed the door and leaned back against it. I tried to convince myself it had all been a dream and not a supernatural manifestation. But I knew it wasn't.

Next morning my father told me that he, too, had had a nightmare in which he stood at my closed bedroom door listening to my screams that a ghost was in the room with me. This was the only indication my father ever gave of being aware of the dark presence that had returned to haunt me.

The following weekend Ralph, my friend from the Psychic Research Society of Australia, came to visit. As we sat discussing the unexplained happenings, he suddenly walked over to the television and held out his hand.

'There's some kind of energy field here,' he stated flatly. 'The air is different.'

I went and stood beside him. I began to move my hand around and became aware of this energy field too. We eventually discerned the energy field was in the form of a large sphere that went through the floor. On impulse we went down to the garage beneath the apartment block and were surprised to find that the *energy sphere* came through the ceiling of the garage from the apartment above.

By now, of course, we had become very intrigued as to what all this meant. Upon returning to my apartment we decided to stand in the energy field to see what would happen.

The air around us started to get warmer.

The warmth gradually subsided as we moved away from the energy field. A quick search of the apartment brought another four *mystery zones* to light. An idea then came to me. I quickly grabbed pen and paper and drew a rough plan of the apartment.

Marking the location of the five energy zones with an 'x', I traced a line from one 'x' to another.

A five-pointed star started to take shape on the paper. The Pentagram. An occult symbol of power and protection.

An unseen malevolent presence. The ghost of a little girl. Psychic attacks. And now, an invisible pentagram. The whole affair was becoming increasingly more bizarre, and I felt that if I were ever to unravel the mystery then only one avenue of investigation remained. That would be a controlled attempt to contact the ghost of the little girl by psychic means - a séance.

At this time, I was attending a psychic development class under the guidance of a young woman called Joan. I told her about the little girl whose ghost I had seen, and she suggested the class visit my apartment as a kind of field trip. None of the others in the class had ever experienced much in the way of the supernatural, and so the visit was arranged for the following weekend.

Everyone arrived on the appointed day, full of expectancy as to what might happen, unaware they were about to be caught in a web of mystery. Joan was the first to arrive and, to pass the time until the others arrived, began browsing through my collection of occult books.

She suddenly backed away from the bookcase with a horrified look on her face.

'You should burn these,' she said, indicating a number of books.

'What's wrong with them?' I asked.

'They're dangerous.'

By this time Ralph had arrived. He was just

as perplexed as I at Joan's reaction to the books. The books she considered dangerous were those containing certain Spells and Rituals of a diabolic nature.

Ralph tried to explain to her that the books were quite harmless just sitting there on the shelf. He said that a dictionary could be considered dangerous also because it contained many words. It only became dangerous when someone rearranged the words to form a curse. It was the same with the books: the Spells were harmless until someone started to read them out loud with the intention of using them on someone. But she would not be convinced.

We positioned an armchair so that it faced the hallway, where all this first started. Joan's father sat back in the chair and closed his eyes. The rest of us went and stood in the five energy fields spread throughout the apartment. Quite suddenly everyone began to speak at once. They were experiencing the same *warm air* phenomena that Ralph and I had experienced.

'I'm starting to get dizzy,' yelled the young girl who was standing within the energy field in the main bedroom. 'It's like I'm rocking back and forth from foot to foot.'

'What do we do?' cried another.

The whole group was now in a state bordering on panic. I'm no psychic, but I could sense that things were getting out of hand.

Joan told everyone to get out of the energy fields immediately. We filed back into the living room and waited for her to offer an explanation as to what was happening.

I asked her what was causing the sensations, and she replied that the spirit force in the apartment was getting hostile and attempting to take possession of us.

Although you can't see it, your body is surrounded by a multi-coloured cloud-like light. The psychic fraternity has always called this light the aura. It is the aura, not the soul, which can be possessed by external spirit forces.

Possessing entities draw off energy from the aura, leaving the hapless victim physically and emotionally exhausted, driving them to commit evil deeds and generally act and behave in a repulsive manner, resembling the creations of imaginative writers.

If you suspect a dangerous entity is attempting to possess you, you should know how to deal with it. This is only common sense. Ascertaining whether or not you are under the influence of some malignant spirit force is not difficult; the effects of possession manifest themselves in the manner described, and by inexplicable depressive moods.

Another way of ascertaining if you are under the influence of a possessing entity is to consult a psychic, though I would caution the reader about approaching them as many so-called gifted psychics provide absolutely no genuine service at all.

Once a possessing entity has attached itself to a person's aura it can only be driven out by persistent application of an occult cleansing ritual. The Cabbalistic Cross Ritual, described in Chapter 5, is just such a ritual.

Joan asked her father to report on what he had discovered. He did not respond. She asked him again. Again no response. I went and stood next to her.

'What's wrong with your father?' I whispered.

She shrugged. 'I'm not sure. I've never seen him like this before.'

Her father suddenly became agitated, his breathing less relaxed. There was, he claimed, a nebulous octopus-like shape taking form in the hallway. A venomous creature, brought into existence out of a luminous green mist. Although we could see nothing in the hallway, we could all sense it. Something *was* there. Something cold and evil.

It began to move towards him.

'No! Go back! Go back!' he cried.

'Call on your Spirit Guides, dad,' said Joan. 'They'll protect you!'

As the minutes passed and nothing happened, we began to fear for his safety. Nervous glances were exchanged.

Had the creature taken possession of him?

'It's gone,' he said softly. 'It's gone now. I've

never seen anything like it before. There was some kind of mass of energy here in the past. I think we had better start the séance as soon as possible.'

A solitary white candle stood at the centre of the small round table around which we were seated, holding hands in the darkened living room. As an aid in contacting the forces at work in the apartment, a young woman in the group volunteered to stand in one of the energy fields for the duration of the séance.

Five minutes had passed when we became aware that something was happening.

The woman who had left the room screamed that something invisible had tried to push her over. Joan asked the woman's husband, an acupuncturist called Owen, to go and bring his wife back into the living room. Once she had returned, the séance continued.

The air around us became ice cold. The girl sitting next to Ralph became so cold she started to shiver. I later learned that while this was happening, Ralph's left arm had become numb and that he had lost all feeling and movement in his arm.

During this time, I began to gradually lose touch with reality. I was aware and yet unaware of those round about me. The sound of Joan's voice brought me back to the here and now. She was describing how she could hear a woman's spirit screaming for help.

The others were getting quite scared, as I don't think any of them had ever experienced anything like this before. I decided to ask Joan a question.

'Tell me about the little girl.'

'All I can tell you is that her name is Ellie.'

Shortly after this we broke from the séance. The girl who had sat next to Ralph was still quite cold, so we wrapped a blanket around her to keep her warm. In the hours that followed we discussed the strange apparition that had appeared in the hallway. Obviously, we concluded, it was a dangerous entity of some kind.

I was advised that the burning of sandalwood incense would create a protective barrier around me with which to keep the beast at bay.

The burning of incense has always been a part of the Occult Sciences. It has a long tradition of magical powers, being used for all kinds of purposes but specifically to make one susceptible to psychic changes deep within one's own mind.

It did not occur to me at the time that all this would be so frightening to the others. The person who did surprise me most by her reactions was Joan. I thought she would have encountered this type of phenomena before, after all she was conducting psychic development classes and gave the impression of being knowledgeable in such matters.

However, she had seemed more scared than the rest of us.

As she left, she warned me the creature would return that night (it did not).

Two days later, I received a visit from a young woman called Raven. She identified herself as being a local psychic who had been contacted by Joan.

As we sat at the very same table that had been used during the séance, Raven explained that Ellie was a restless spirit lured by the creature (seen by Joan's father) into a kind of *psychic web.*

She also described three entities who had suddenly appeared in the courtyard. The enigmatic mysteries that had swept into my life were now joined by yet another. All three entities were dressed in black, silent and staring up at my living room window.

Raven assured me that I had nothing to fear from these three strangers, and that Ellie would never again return to haunt me. The creature was gone, I realised, and with it the ghost of little Ellie.

As for Raven, maybe the three entities in black took her away with them, because I never saw or heard from her again.

Yet there were further mysteries to come.

For me, there would be many encounters with the supernatural and ritual workings. But not just that. A fallen angel lay in wait.

The Darkest Unknown

On 31 October 1992 three people were drawn together to call forth a Spirit out of Legend. I was one of those people. For me it began two weeks earlier when I received an interstate phone call from a young girl living in a rural township, which by itself was nothing extraordinary. What was extraordinary was her claim that she had received a strange psychic message that she must come to my home and work a ritual to Astaroth.

The dark lord of many legions, Astaroth's power is eternal and goes beyond life into the darkest unknown. In his true form, Astaroth manifests as a dark heartbeat: *darkness with the sound of a heart beating.*

It seemed too fantastic to believe. I had never been particularly convinced by demonstrations of alleged psychic messages from Spirit Guides and the like. Years of attending various psychic development classes and conversations with alleged clairvoyants had left me more than a little skeptical about such things. But, however unbelievable it was, I felt compelled to find out what really lay behind this odd phone call from a girl I had never met. A girl whose name was Julie.

A few nights after our initial contact, Julie called me again to discuss the ritual. She was joking and in good spirits. We discussed the actual mechanics of the ritual and the layout of the room in which the ritual would be worked.

About halfway through the conversation, Julie heard a noise. A strange scraping sound in the next room. She stopped talking and listened. It came again. A prolonged sound like fingernails being dragged across the wall. She began to experience the usual reaction to the presence of something unseen: fear.

There was a dull thud on the other end of the line. A vase had been knocked to the floor by an invisible hand. The sound of a beating heart filled the room.

'He's here!' she screamed down the phone. 'Astaroth is here!'

She dissolved into total hysteria, crying uncontrollably. The bright, cheerful girl of a moment ago was now an emotional wreck. This was not just some act being staged for my benefit. I tried to calm her. I assured her there was nothing to fear, and not to be afraid.

I had two interesting reactions to this event. I was genuinely afraid. My first thought was to hang up and forget about the whole thing. Secondly, while I was listening to Julie's description of what was happening to her, I felt a strange sensation like pins-and-needles moving up my body from the base of the spine.

Thanks to that wonderful thing known as 'hindsight', I can now review that night with a bit more clarity and see things that escaped me while I was living it. I realised that my reactions to the situation may have been more auto-suggestive than real.

It was Halloween. Julie and I sat drinking wine in my living room. Ralph was also present. As we sat discussing the varied strange events that had happened in our lives, I began to sense the presence of unseen forces round about us. There was an air of expectancy in the room. Outside, the air was still. Not even a bird call.

As we talked on, Ralph remarked on the fact that most witches work their rituals in the nude. Julie asked him if that's how he wanted it today. He quickly said no!

I felt a slight tug in the area of my solar plexus. A spirit had entered me. It was time to begin. A small round table was carried into the centre of the room. For the most part we all remained silent during this time. Our thoughts were on what the Ritual would bring. Curtains were drawn, candles lit and three glasses of wine placed upon the table.

'How do I look?' Julie asked. She had changed into the loose, flowing white dress the psychic message had instructed her to wear.

'Like a sacrificial virgin,' I said. 'Now, let's get started.'

We raised our glasses in a toast to Astaroth.

After drinking the wine we all joined hands. Three working as one to give purpose to our intent.

Ralph's hands were cold to the touch. He was afraid. I shot him a look out of the corner of my eye. I half expected to see him break out in a cold sweat. It was uncharacteristic of him to express a fear of the unknown. I feared that he might affect the outcome of the Ritual.

'I think you should begin,' Julie said quietly. 'I feel the time is right to begin.'

Encouraged by this, I intoned a prayer to Astaroth asking for his help in the Ritual. I thanked him for all his help to others in days long ago, and for being with us this day.

As my voice fell silent and the candles burned, the anticipation began to mount. My breathing became heavier, and a tingling sensation rushed through me as the unseen forces round about us overwhelmed me with their power and authority.

The ritual proceeded. Julie made herself comfortable upon a makeshift bed on the floor. I went and stood at the head of the bed and began using hand gestures to entice Astaroth into Julie's body. Julie lay completely silent and still, as if in a very deep sleep.

Then suddenly she spoke: 'To you I give my body,' she sighed. 'Take me. Use me. And in return, reward me.'

She fell silent, and a sudden concentration of power seemed to gather around us. With it there came awareness. A sense of timeless darkness - ageless, eternal. Ralph turned to me, wide-eyed. The power wavered and died. It was done.

Later, as we discussed what had happened, Ralph admitted he had been a little nervous the whole time. I told him his hands had been as cold as ice.

'Really? How odd, I felt rather hot the whole time. One thing is certain though, it's been a very interesting afternoon.'

It had indeed, I thought.

Chapter 2

THE WITCHING CIRCLE

The first full moon after Midsummer's Night hangs in the night sky above a wooded hollow. A naked young girl lies outstretched on an altar, her loose blonde hair rippling over her shoulders and across the cold altar stones. Her pale flesh bathed in the glow of the full moon above. Her breasts rise and fall to the fear inside her, as hooded figures draw close to the altar and a low-pitched chant begins to fill the night air.

Standing before her, the Coven Master takes up the chant as, with head bowed, an assistant hands him the sacrificial knife, its blade shining in the silver moonlight. From out of the dark wood another figure appears. The figure is leading a goat, which he takes to the side of the altar as the priest begins his litany.

He calls out a list of demonic names and to them he addresses his earnest plea for them to bear witness to what is about to take place.

'Astaroth, help us!' he intones. *'Demons, Dagon, Azazel, Pan help us! Asmodeus, we beseech thee! We are gathered here in thy honour, O Great God, Baal! We offer unto thee*

the body of the virgin, so that we may live eternally in the darkness of thy womb.'

Then, with knife raised high, he walks slowly towards the goat and, with a quick, neat thrust, he slits its throat.

An expectant hush falls as three hooded figures step forward to catch the blood in a golden chalice and pass it around the coven, each of whom takes a sip, then bows his head.

Finally, it is the Coven Master's turn. He raises the chalice, drinks part of its contents and uses the still-warm blood to draw numerous occult symbols on the belly of the naked girl. An excited wail rises up from the coven and is quickly stilled.

So begins a typical witchcraft ceremony. Or perhaps I should say, Hollywood's idea of a typical witchcraft ceremony. The truth is, most witches are involved in rather mundane things like ceremonies to ensure that the sun comes up every morning. You can't help feeling that there must be more to it than this.

There are two sides, or faces, to witchcraft: the pagan worship of Nature, and the manipulative side, that of deliberately influencing chance and coincidence for one's own end.

What Witches Do

The cornerstone of witchcraft is the coven. A

coven is just a fancy name for a group of people who like to get together every so often, take all their clothes off and dance about in a circle, in the open air. It is lead by a Coven Master. The purpose of the coven is to build magical energy amongst its members to achieve the coven's common objectives.

Covens hold great feasts on certain nights each year: 2 February (Candlemas), 30 April (Walpurgis Night), 1 August (Lammas), and 31 October (Halloween).

These four dates are the main witch Sabots of the year. They are special nights on which white witches gather to celebrate their devotion to the moon goddess Diana, and the goat-footed god of fertility, Pan, indulging in drink, laughter, love and song.

The more interesting covens, on the other hand, indulge in an orgy of wickedness where all the instincts are given free reign. The dark forces, pleased by the perversions performed for them, then pursue the tasks asked of them by the participants.

Welcome to the Coven

There are various forms of secret initiation ceremonies, depending on the type of coven one seeks to join. In most instances the initiate is a woman though, in some cases, a man will be initiated into the coven.

The Coven Master enters the room and draws a magic circle on the floor. The spirits of the North are called upon to witness the ceremony with the words, '*I summon, serve and call Ye up Mighty Ones of the North to guard the Circle and to witness our rites.*'

The initiate is led naked to the centre of the circle with her hands tied behind her back and blindfolded.

At the centre of the circle she repeats a solemn vow, and then she is presented to each member of the coven who greet her with a kiss. She is then introduced to the spirits of the four cardinal points.

She then kneels in the centre of the circle and is asked what she most desires, and answers '*To serve the Old Ones*'.

Finally she is asked if she realises that, before she can be accepted, her body must first be purified, and answers '*I do*'.

She is then whipped forty times across the quivering flesh of her naked behind.

The blindfold is removed with the words, '*So be it*'.

Her bonds are removed with the words, '*Now you are free*'.

Once again she is presented to each member of the coven, who greet her with a kiss. The coven is now free to spend the evening in whatever way they wish.

Anyone Can Be a Witch

Contrary to popular belief, not all witches belong to covens. I certainly don't, though I do live in close proximity to an area of parkland once used by a coven who held its meetings during the Second World War.

Many work alone and with just as good results using the Magic Power of witchcraft as if they were working with a group. They use the power of their imagination, focused by concentration and belief, to cast Spells.

There is nothing special that you have to be, or no-one special you have to know, in order for you to work witchcraft. Those who would wish you not to know how easy it is to use the Magic Power of witchcraft have fostered this commonly held belief.

As you sit reading this, the essence of that Power is sinking deep into your Inner Mind. This chapter has been written in a special way. No matter whether you believe me or not, the magic behind the words is awakening racial memories of a time long ago when this Power was free to every man and woman who sought it. Using this magical power is simplicity itself.

In detail, I'll be explaining how to do it later in this book.

The Circle of Protection

In Chapter 3 you will learn how to create your

personal witching circle in which to cast Spells. As you work your magic, you will begin to *glow* in a metaphysical sense. Spirits can see this glow and are drawn to it, and some will try to mislead you.

You can protect yourself from this by taking a handful of salt and, walking in a clockwise direction, sprinkle the salt around the perimeter of the circle, all the while saying: *'Let this space, be a safe and magical place'.*

It's a good idea to work this Ritual on a regular basis.

The Sign of the Elder Gods

The pentagram (five-pointed star) is another tool used by both witches and magicians to keep evil forces at bay. The more complicated forms of magic require the magician to create a Cabalistic circle of protection. In this circle a pentagram is visualised at each of the cardinal points, joined one to the other by a fiery circle with the magician at its centre.

However, there is more to it than this, of course.

The protection of the four archangels is requested, along with the visualisation of the archangels and the elemental forces associated with them. In detail, I'll be explaining how to do it later in this book.

The pentagram represents man - the five points being his head, two arms and two legs. Inverted it becomes the symbol of Baphomet, the Goat of a Thousand Young.

Now, to understand what Baphomet represents, I need to give you a little lesson on the Knights Templar, a debased Christian sect that practised occult Rituals.

King Phillipe of France had them burnt at the stake in the 14th century for worshipping Baphomet - an idol with the head and feet of a goat, the breasts of a woman, and the wings of an angel.

Inverted, the pentagram becomes the symbol of Baphomet - the five points being two horns, two ears, and the beard.

Love, Lust and Witchcraft

Witches and witchcraft have long been associated with the search for love. A powerful Love Spell, still secretly practised today, required the warlock of medieval times to watch for a crescent or waning moon between 11pm and midnight.

Before casting the spell he would write, on parchment, the name of the young girl he desired to attract, and draw a circle around it. As soon as he saw the moon, he would seek out the brightest star in the night sky and recite a solemn conjuration so powerful it was believed capable of drawing any young girl the warlock desired to him.

The conjuration was repeated three times and the parchment burned.

The ashes were placed in the warlock's left shoe and were left there until the young girl came to him.

Another powerful Spell, designed to arouse love and passion in another, required the warlock to make a figure of wax to represent the woman whose company he desired above all else.

The preliminaries included burning frankincense, and the solemn lighting of two candles.

The figure of wax, on which were inscribed the names of assorted demons, was passed back and forth through the fumes, while reciting the following conjuration:

'I conjure and command thee, thou spirits, who have the power to disturb the hearts of women! By Him who created thee and by this image, I conjure thee this night into my presence, so I may have the power to compel whomsoever I desire to love me.'

After this the figure of wax was taken to a secluded place and buried.

The warlock of medieval times did not confine his witchery to the securing of love alone; he also lusted after buried treasure and its possessions.

The Black Pullet

One of the most enduring occult legends of riches obtained through the application of magical formulae is related in *The Black Pullet,* a handbook of magic written in 1744.

Imagine if you will Egypt in the 18th Century. A young officer is sent on an expedition to the Pyramids. The party of explorers lunch in the shadow of the great stone mountains of the desert, and are attacked by a horde of Arabs.

The comrades of the young officer are slain, and he himself is left for dead upon the ground. On returning to consciousness, he surrenders himself to the immediate anticipation of his end, and delivers a farewell address to the setting sun. A stone is rolled back in the Pyramid, and a venerable old man issues forth.

The old man does not fail to discover the corpses that are strewn about the desert, or to identify their country of origin.

When the young officer in his turn is examined, the ancient man takes pity on him and gives him a magical liqueur that puts the wounded man back on his feet. He follows the old man into the Pyramid and discovers a world of magic.

There are vast halls and endless galleries, subterranean chambers piled high with treasures, apparitions of blazing lamps and legions of familiar spirits.

Here, also, is *The Black Pullet*. It is a supernatural version of Aladdin with an inner meaning of Astaroth. The sage himself proves to be the sole heir of the ancient magi and is, himself, in quest of an heir for he feels he is about to pass away.

In time the French officer, seeing that his protector possesses a talisman that confers immediate proficiency in all tongues, is instructed in the powers and wonders of twenty-two talismanic figures and magical rings, as well as in the secret of the manufacture of *The Black Pullet*.

After these instructions, and in spite of many prayers, the Old Man of the Pyramids expires upon a sofa, while his apprentice in the esoteric arts swoons at the feet of his mentor.

In due course, accompanied by the familiar spirits that have been transferred to his service, laden with treasures, and with the ashes of the sage in a costly urn, the French officer returns to his native country and spends his days in experiments with *The Black Pullet*.

Such is the legend of *The Black Pullet* and how one may acquire riches through the application of magical rites and ceremonies.

The Magic of Herbs

Herbs have always been a staple item in the witch's world of chants, spells and rituals. They have a long occult tradition, being used for all kinds of weird and wonderful purposes. The historical record shows that they were part of the occult sciences amongst the Ancient Egyptians, Celts, Druids, Romans and Greeks.

Herbs can be obtained in one of two ways. From the countryside where they grow in abundance, or ready-packed for sale in occult supply stores.

Witches have also been known to employ the humble lemon in their spell casting. A traditional formula for ascertaining if the man on a woman's mind is going to be hers or not is the following.

Carry all day in a pocket or purse two lemon peels. One peel can be put in the purse, the other in a pocket - or each peel in a separate pocket. At night before retiring to bed, the woman rubs the legs of the bed with the peels thinking intently of the man.

She then places the peels under her pillow and, that night, if she is to have him, he will appear in a dream. If no dream comes he is not to be hers.

Out of the Night

The art and practice of witchcraft goes hand in hand with eerie legends of mysterious, evil creatures that were seen by the light of a Full Moon.

These legends have existed through the centuries and are as old as man. It is difficult to separate the two. They are all part of the same thing: the unknown world of supernatural forces.

The most enduring of all these legends of evil is that of the mediaeval vampires living in the remote regions of Transylvania who, in order to sustain their monstrous existence, would leave their tombs at midnight to drink the blood of young virgins.

A girl, once bitten, would become a virgin of the undead and, her eyes burning with a dark desire, was forever more drawn back to the vampire's embrace.

The only way to kill a vampire was to drive a sharp, pointed stake through its heart. After this, the body of the vampire had to be taken to a place where three ways met, and then buried.

In the old days those who had committed suicide, or those who had been executed for any kind of witchcraft, were buried at a crossing. Crossings were also considered as ideal places to summon Satan, or start toward a sabot.

Let us not forget that in every legend there is an element of truth.

The Fear of Witchcraft

Most people are paranoid about the fact that

you can use witchcraft either to gain control over them or place a curse upon their heads, and will know that sympathetic magic requires either an item of clothing or a photo to make it work. It is for this reason that no-one will willingly hand over, or send you, anything which could in some way be used to work magic against them.

The basis of sympathetic magic is that there is a connection between an object and a symbol.

For example, make a doll in the likeness of someone you don't like, stick pins in it and the victim gets stabbing pains in his back. Or gather together hair and nail clippings, burn them and the person in question gets a fever.

However, it is not always used to do something unpleasant. The best way to win the love of a young girl is to chant an incantation three times over an apple, give the fruit to the young girl to eat, and she will surely come to you.

The best example of sympathetic magic in witchcraft is the mandrake plant. A rather mysterious plant, its main use in the Middle Ages was as an aphrodisiac due to its shape, which resembles a certain part of the male anatomy.

The powdered root of the mandrake was burned over a fire with some of the witch's pubic hair. At the same time, the witch's lustful desires were spoken, invoking a demon to draw the desired person to the witch's embrace.

Occult tradition has it that you can't harvest the mandrake plant in the normal way, as the scream it gives as it leaves the ground will kill you or drive you mad. The shriek is supposedly the cry of jealous spirits who dwell within. Instead, you tie it to a dog's collar and, when out of earshot, whistle the dog to come to you.

Witchcraft Made Easy

During my twenty plus years of studying and practising the occult sciences, I have come to find that much witchcraft is unnecessarily complicated. Witchcraft is an act of celebration and freedom, and to me it seems pointless that it should get bogged down with rules and regulations.

However, even when you reach the point when you begin to realise that much of the paraphernalia associated with witchcraft, e.g. candles, incense and so forth, can be dispensed with, you will find that the moon still holds sway over certain things.

The ancient witch cults knew this and timed their activities to the different phases of the moon.

Positive magic is worked from the first quarter until a full moon, and black magic from the last quarter until a new moon.

The more things change, the more they stay the same.

Chapter 3

THE FIERY SERPENT

You have a Power within you that can be woken. It is what the Ancient Avatars of the Mystic East use to call 'the Fiery Serpent', 'the Great Body of Radiance' or 'the Immutable Light'. It is the same Power that you can now use to work any Magic you want.

You may have expected at this stage that you would be told to transform your living room into something resembling an old, gothic room and to obtain a cauldron in which to boil bat's wing and eye of newt, or to mumble strange chants as you indulge in a spot of blood drinking. Such occult paraphernalia and activities are not only out of date, but also totally unnecessary to make your Magic Power work for you.

The first thing is to find a place where you can create a witching circle. Preparations are simple, but you need to ensure there will be silence with no interruptions.

First, make a physical space to stand in without being obstructed or cluttered. That means that when you stand at the centre of your cleared area, you can stretch your hands and arms out all around you.

This is your personal Witching Circle.

If you wish you can burn a stick of incense and have the room illuminated by candles placed at the four cardinal points.

Until you are confident in your power to keep mischievous spirits at bay, mark a circle of protection on the floor in salt.

The Seven Doorways

There are seven mystic power centres (or doorways) within the human body. It is from these 'doorways' that your Magic Power flows into the physical world to work on the minds of other people, and to manoeuvre chance and coincidence to bring you what you seek.

Each of the seven mystic power centres relates to a specific area of your life, and all seven centres must be pulsating in rhythm as you begin your journey into the Invisible World of Magic and Witchcraft. The Ritual below is designed to awaken your fiery serpent and to get all seven mystic power centres working in unison.

You Can Awaken Your Magic Power

Here now is a Ritual to summon the magic power within you. This requires only a few minutes of your time each day. Remember you also need privacy. When witches work their rituals, they work naked. The absence of clothing leaves them completely free and unrestricted, not only in body but also in mind and spirit, and this is how you should work the Spells and Rituals that follow.

Stand at the centre of your witching circle, with your feet about twenty-four inches apart. Face north. Move your hands and arms upward and outward, fingers straight and palms forward, so that you are standing in the shape of an 'X'.

Close your eyes and take ten deep breaths.

Lift your chin, inhale and arch your back as much as you can. Begin to breathe out, straighten up, and bring your hands slowly down to your sides.

Take three deep breaths after your hands reach your sides, bring your feet together and open your eyes.

End of Ritual.

When this Ritual has been completed, you have made a very definite contact with the magic power of witchcraft. Your life will never again be the same.

Whenever a specific area of your life is in need of help, work the whole of the Ritual and, as you finish taking the three breaths, cast whatever Spell is appropriate to your desire. It is the Spell that draws out your power and sends it on its way.

For easy reference, think of the entire Ritual as 'the awakening of magic power' up to the point where you open your eyes again. I shall be referring to that description later in this book. The instructions will say, 'Awaken your magic power' and this tells you that you should prepare for the Ritual and carry it out from beginning to end.

Note: If your doctor advises you that deep breathing is dangerous for you; or if at any time during this magic working you become dizzy or see spots before your eyes, do not continue.

Here you should know about different sensations that often accompany the awakening of your magic power. I mention it because you may be worried by it until you are told it is perfectly normal.

As you bring your hands down, a tingling or warmth, or both, may be felt around them. A strong itching or tickling may begin in your forehead, well below the skin. These are all signs that your magic power is flooding to the surface.

Before you have been doing it for a full week, the Ritual will take you out of yourself and into a state of well-being that lasts. You can be confident that anything and everything that happens to you during and after the Ritual are to your benefit.

Seeing Your Magic Power

Perhaps you are thinking 'How can something I can't see possibly help me?' You are about to learn how to see this magical energy which is normally invisible to the naked eye, and it will take just a few minutes of your time.

Once this happens, you will be above any doubt, and no amount of argument or ridicule from others who have yet to understand will ever be able to convince you that invisible occult forces do not exist.

I learnt this particular technique during my days at the Psychic Research Society of Australia. No special equipment is required for this simple psychic experience.

Switch off the TV and radio. Place an ordinary padded kitchen chair in the centre of your witching circle. Once your chair is positioned, darken the room by drawing the drapes or hanging a blanket at the window. Ideally, the room should be dim enough so that you cannot read the fine print of a newspaper.

Now, arrange a single light to shine gently over your shoulder so that you are able to see your hands in front of you.

Awaken your magic power.

Sit down in your chair and relax. Make yourself comfortable with your back straight, but not stiff. Tuck your buttocks into the back of the chair so that your spine is upright, with your chin held level without straining to hold the position.

Place your feet flat on the floor, almost touching.

Lay your hands in one of two ways, whichever feels most comfortable, either palms upward on your thighs or palms downward on your lap.

You are now ready to begin.

Hold up your right hand so that the light shining gently over your shoulder illuminates it, and bring your fingers together so that your thumb and forefinger are touching, in the shape of an 'O'.

Now separate your fingers a little, moving the tips a fraction of an inch apart. Look past your fingers at a spot in front of you. Between your fingers, a hazy light should be visible. This is your magic power circulating around you.

Earth, Air, Fire and Water

Witches have always recognised the magical powers that exist in the four elements of earth, air, fire and water, and how these powers could be used in everyday life. Now you, too, can use these very same powers to bring you what you seek.

Enter your witching circle. Face North. Awaken the magic power within you and, keeping your eyes closed, visualise a golden square directly in front of you.

This is the symbol of Earth.

Using your own words, thank the spirits of Earth for all their help to others in days gone by.

Thank them for being with you on this day and at this hour. Remove the image from your mind.

Face East. Visualise a blue circle in front of you.

This is the symbol of Air.

Thank the spirits of the Air for all their help to others in days gone by. Thank them for being with you on this day and at this hour. Remove the image from your mind.

Face South. Visualise a red triangle in front of you.

This is the symbol of Fire.

Thank the spirits of Fire for all their help to others in days gone by. Thank them for being with you on this day and at this hour.

Remove the image from your mind.

Face West. Visualise a silver crescent.

This is the symbol of Water.

Thank the spirits of Water for all their help to others in days gone by. Thank them for being with you on this day and at this hour. Remove the image from your mind and face North again. Say the following:

'These hands, this mind and this body shall be a channel through which power will flow'.

Open your eyes and go about your daily affairs.

Practice this Rite daily. Get the Magic habit. Set up those harmonic vibrations that are so essential to the occult sciences. You will probably find that you have a natural affinity with the Elemental Force associated with your astrological sign.

Anytime you feel like putting a triumphant emphasis onto a magical working, or you wish to make absolutely certain that a particular Spell or Ritual is totally successful, align yourself with the Elemental Forces. It will add that final whammy of force and direction to your efforts.

A Thank You Email

Paul C., an ardent student of the occult arts, sent me an email.

'First, I want to thank you for making yourself available to answer questions online,' he wrote. 'I truly appreciate it. Here's my situation.

'I have several health problems I'm using an occult ritual to heal myself. It seems to be working somewhat for me. It appeals to the Spirit Beings *Zoroel* and *Sabriel*, who govern health, for healing. Naturally, I'm thankful for their assistance.

'I do a self-hypnosis/relaxation induction and

then perform the ritual. I feel this is helping me. Somehow, I intuit that my progress is artificially slow, like I somehow am standing in my own way. I've tried many things over the past few years to help.

'My question is: Are you aware of any ways of strengthening a ritual?'

I replied to his email, explaining that the simplest way of strengthening a ritual was to align with the elemental forces of Earth, Air, Fire and Water. I suggested he should continue with the relaxation technique and add the elemental ritual to his magical workings. I ended the email by asking him to keep me informed of his progress.

Another email arrived from Paul a few days later.

'Since you asked,' he wrote. 'Last night I performed the elemental rite you sent me for the first time. It was a very positive experience! I put off starting it for a couple of days, as I could not find my trusty compass to make sure I was facing the four directions. I did a best guess even though my sense of direction could have been slightly off.

'Amazingly, I felt a powerful sense of friendship and rapport with each of the four elemental forces and spirits as I spoke the words. I just let myself be infused with this feeling and considered it "legit" even though the critical factor wants to dismiss it as imagination.'

Paul's e-mail went on to say that performing the ritual gave him a very strong case of what he called the *psychic hiss*.

'You know that strong hiss you hear in your ears and feel resonating from where the base of your skull meets the top of your neck,' he wrote. 'Physically, I felt a strong sense of well-being as I finished the ritual. I consider it a successful effort. I'd better stop there. My enthusiasm might get me too far ahead of myself. There's still a way to go yet.

'Your suggestion seems to be a very helpful one, I'll keep you posted on the progress. Thanks!'

Using Witchcraft to Smooth Your Path Through Life

If you have diligently studied and practised awakening your magic power and calling forth the spirits of the four cardinal points, you are ready to assimilate the magic of elemental witchcraft power.

This advanced work is suitable only if you have developed a harmonic relationship with the Elemental Forces, and if you have succeeded in awakening your magic power.

Enter your witching circle and face North, South, East or West. The direction that you face will depend on your desire.

The correlation between elemental forces

and desires is as follows:

Earth: Financial security and stability. Practical areas of life. Work and career. Material desires. *Air:* Love and friendship. Travel. Social activities. Subtle changes. Intellectual pursuits. *Fire:* Passion and desire. Psychic protection. Energy. Willpower. Removal of conflict. Transformation. Destruction. *Water:* Health and wellbeing. Emotions. Women. Magic. Secrets. Intuition. Moon. Hopes and dreams.

Awaken your magic power and, as you finish taking the three breaths, visualise an elemental symbol directly in front of you.

Now, enlarge the symbol until it is several feet high and pulsating with magical power. See it as clearly as you can. Imagine you are bathed in its mystic light.

Try and actually breathe in this mystic light. Imagine it circulating within you.

Now call forth the spirits of the symbol and ask them for help in achieving your desire.

Spend a few minutes thinking about whatever it is that you seek in the way of happiness and peace of mind. Say a simple 'thank you' to the spirits and go about your daily affairs. Repeat daily.

Chapter 4

FIVE DYNAMIC SPELLS TO BRING YOU WHAT YOU SEEK

In Chapter 3 you learned that the magic power of witchcraft can be woken through the study and practice of the Fiery Serpent Ritual. If you never learned another thing about the Occult World, the knowledge that you already possess marks you as a genuine witch.

But there is more, much more. Obtaining money through the use of Magic Spells and Rituals is just one more amazing secret that is revealed to you in the pages of this book.

How to Cast Spells That Really Work

Spells are the fun part of what we call witchcraft; simple gestures, uttered words, seemingly illogical actions, all frowned upon by the scientific mind, nevertheless make strange and wonderful things happen for the person who casts them. The casting of Spells is based upon the arcane belief that to speak a desire is to cause the desire to be fulfilled.

When it comes to spell casting, there's always a chance of first time success if the desire is strong, though it usually does take time and practice to achieve results. Spells draw out the Magic Power within you and focus it dynamically to shape your future.

Get involved with the Spell, focus on the details. In that way you will turn it from a simple, unemotional act, into a genuine Spell of Power and Force.

Use these Spells to obtain only one desire at a time. If you go after a whole string of desires, the magical power is spread thinly over all of them and will take longer. Better to achieve one at a time in order of importance.

If you find yourself being constantly interrupted when you attempt to cast a Spell, you should know that occult forces are the cause. Probably you should attempt some other means of obtaining what you seek (take a look at another Spell), or reconsider your actions.

Thank You Letter #1

'I never thought I would see the day when I would be using witchcraft to help me. I am not particularly religious, I have an open mind, but my life has improved over the last three months since I followed your advice. I am writing to tell you how grateful I am. I know the Spells work.

'I have had lots of small sums of money to keep me in food and clothes, which I had never bargained for. And the man I want is with me and loves me.'

Signed: S. A., England.

Practical Witchcraft

Having now defined our subject, let us progress to the practical uses for which it can be employed.

Let us first take a look at Spells that will appeal to many readers, namely Spells to bring money.

You will not find a bundle of cash in an old shoebox or win the lottery by using these Spells. They are designed to bring small but sustained increases in spending money.

By the way, if you are in the least bit worried that the practical application of witchcraft in some way breaks one of the basic arcane laws, don't be. Let me assure you that witches won't admit that they are using witchcraft to do what everyone would want to use it for - to bring money, power and sex.

The Green Candle Spell

This Spell has proven extremely successful. It is concerned with bringing moderate amounts of money to meet financial needs. Before beginning, write down on a piece of paper what bills need paying or what you want the money for. Keep it simple.

After darkness has fallen, enter your witching circle and light a single green candle. If you wish you can burn a stick of incense and have soft music playing. Put out all lights except the candle and read your piece of paper once more.

Awaken your magic power and then close your eyes and see exactly what it is that you want, e.g. see the money appearing in your hands. Get involved with the money. Use your imagination to touch and feel the money. Know that it is real.

Having visualised for a few minutes, open your eyes and gaze into the candle flame.

Say the magical word 'OM' seven times, slowly. Close your eyes again and visualise the money in your hands.

Now, sit back and wait for the money to come to you.

You will notice the use of the colour green for this Spell. Green is the traditional colour used by witches in money matters. Green is the colour of Mother Nature and is also the colour of paper money; dollar bills are green.

Thank You Letter #2

'I have been much intrigued by the many different ideas regarding getting one's desires via metaphysical means. You may be interested to know that following your advice resulted in a check for $1,000 from a brother I saw twenty-seven years ago for about one hour! Time before had been 1946 or '47 - extent of our correspondence has been yearly Xmas Cards. He lives in the Southeastern USA.

'Since I need funds for a new car and extensive property upgrading and repairs - I shall keep trying! Will let you know what happens! Thanks again.'

Signed: H. P., USA.

Earth Magic

Gnomes are the elemental spirits of the earth. One occult belief is that gnomes are the guardians of buried treasure and the bringers of gold. Their essence can be found in the earth, wood and metals.

This Spell will help you to enlist their aid in your affairs.

Before you begin, go outside and pick up a pinch of earth and take it inside with you. Enter your witching circle. Face North, and sprinkle the soil on the floor in front of you.

That small and simple gesture forges a bond between you and the gnomes, and adds power to the Spell.

Awaken your magic power. Imagine a golden square directly in front of you. Now enlarge the image until it is several feet high and pulsating with mystic force. See it as clearly as you can.

Imagine yourself bathed in its mystic light. Try and actually breathe in this light. Imagine it circulating within you.

Now, in your mind, pretend that you are reaching into the golden square. Feel around inside until your hands touch two moneybags, bulging with gold coins.

Pick the bags up and bring them out from within the golden square. Feel the coins with your mind, get involved with the coins, imagine they're real.

End the Spell by thanking the gnomes for their help.

Repeat for seven consecutive days, or until the money arrives, or until you are stopped from casting the Spell, whichever happens first.

Spell Brings Needed Money

This particular case history was told to me over the telephone, so I will have to relate it using my own words.

Laura D. was by no means rich, and when she received a phone bill for $300 she had no idea where she could get the money. She was at her wit's end.

So when I suggested that she use the Earth Forces to draw money to her, she was only too happy to give it a try.

She followed my instructions.

One week later, Laura's mother-in-law came

to visit and handed her an envelope. A gift, she told Laura. It contained exactly $300 in cash.

A miracle? Laura certainly thought so, but I knew it was just the proper application of Elemental Magic.

The Earth Forces worked for Laura and they will work for you, too.

The Devil's Treasurer

This is a very potent Black Magic Spell to bring money. If Black Magic didn't work, there would be no reason for me to include this Spell in this chapter or for you to try it. But Black Magic really works.

It's not the old-fashioned kind with bats and black cats, but an entirely new magical system based on principles thousands of years old that, under the correct conditions, works every time.

This Spell is the result of years of research into arcane magical texts and documents. All the confusing parts of the old texts have been discarded.

The remaining wisdom has been sorted out, de-fantasised and re-integrated into a proven system that works. This Spell can yield regular financial gains if performed correctly.

Enter your witching circle and face East. Awaken your magic power. Light a gold candle and hold a one dollar bill (or one pound coin) in your right hand. Recite a short prayer to the

Spirit Astaroth.

Astaroth is one of seventy-two Spirits listed in the *Lemegeton,* a four-part handbook of magic also called *The Lesser Key of Solomon*, written before 1500 AD. The four parts are *Goetia*, derived from a Greek word meaning 'witchcraft,' *Theurgia Goetia*, the Pauline Art, and the *Amadel*.

Thank Astaroth for all his help to others in days gone by. Thank him also for being with you on this day and at this hour, and ask for his kindness and favour at this time.

Sit quietly for a few moments before summoning the Spirit Astaroth to you, using your own words. It is at this moment that the Spirit Astaroth will manifest or make known his presence in the room with you, and you must speak of whatever it is you want in the way of ready cash.

You may converse with Astaroth in words and gestures, or silently if you wish. You must get involved.

When you are ready, give thanks to Astaroth and bid him farewell.

Keep the money in your pocket or purse. Don't spend it for at least ten days or until the money appears, whichever occurs first.

This is a very personal magical working. You conjure Astaroth in your own way and with your own words. Your emotions will be stirred by this magical working.

This ancient money rite is particularly effective in bringing 'smallish amounts' of money at frequent intervals. It may be $50 one day, $30 the next, $100 the week after, all from the most unexpected sources. Use it regularly and it could solve your financial worries for life.

I would suggest you cast this Spell on a Wednesday, between 10pm and 11pm, about one week after the New Moon.

I once knew a young man who scored a handsome windfall after I told him about the motivating powers of the Spirit Astaroth. One weekend he visited a large casino to try his luck at roulette. He placed his bets and, much to his amazement, won over $1000.

Thank You Letter #3

'One thing leads to another and there seems to be new developments every day of my life.

'Yes Carl, a week after doing the Money Spell, a lady gave me a check for $100 in sympathy of my stolen Tape Deck to buy a small one, and the Personnel Manager also gave me $50 as a gift.

'After the ten days I got the money used in the Spell and had it in my purse. I eventually spent it as I didn't know whether to keep it as a magnet in my purse or spend it. However, my Bank Manager decided to loan me $1000.

'I will have to do it again this New Moon, but

tell me what to do with the money used in the Spell? Keep it or spend it?'

Signed: John T., USA.

The Black Candle of Love

The occult practitioners of ages past were the matchmakers of their day. Almost without exception, every small village had its resident *wise woman* dispensing love spells and philters of various kinds to those in search of true love. No occult book would be complete without information on how to win the love of another.

For the female witch intent on seduction, cast this Love Spell before coming into the presence of the man concerned.

Enter your witching circle. Awaken your magic power. Burn a black candle and think of the person to be spellbound. After a few minutes, gaze into the candle flame and say:

'Listen, O Mighty and Powerful Ancient One, He whose appearance is that of a burning pillar of fire. Ancient and Powerful One, I require you, Who hath dominion over such things to draw close to you the heart and soul of (Person's Name).

From this moment forth, I charge you to never once loosen your hold upon them. By He whose mouth ever flameth, You are required to do as I command. Let (Person's Name) *never think of another for his/her soul has now faded from within.* (Person's Name) *is now bound to my will, until the stars fall from the heavens.'*

You will, of course, have been using the appropriate pronoun where the Spell says 'her' or 'his'.

Repeat this Spell daily until results are obtained. It's best to cast this Spell on a night when the Moon is full.

Thank You Letter #4

'I have for the past two years really liked a man in our village. He is everything women go for. I am the hairdresser in the village. One day I decided to do some trickery on him, knowing full well he did not fancy me at all. I did the *Black Candle Spell*.

'Well, needless to say, it worked and if you knew this man you would have said it was almost impossible. Anyway, we went away for a day and night in a hotel. He made love to me twice! Thank you!'

Signed: S.U., England.

The Magic Power of Chants

Ask any witch worth their broomstick and they will tell you that certain sounds (chants) create unique magical vibrations. They will also tell you that these magical vibrations seek similar vibrations within the Astral World, becoming a single creative force of energy that goes to work to make a physical manifestation of its power.

This physical manifestation is called Magic.

The secret chant I will soon reveal to you is so effective that it should be used with caution. I discovered it in a long out of print book of Spells and Rituals. I began using it, idly, without thinking and, as I did, a strange sequence of events followed that even I am at a loss to explain.

In the days and weeks ahead, everything I wanted I received with this secret chant: new friends, rare books, money and more.

I felt a strange sensation envelop me, a feeling of power and protection.

The chant should be spoken aloud in a sort of 'up and down' rhythm. Before you begin saying the chant, practise aloud by counting from one to seven in the same voice that you will use when using the chant, to influence chance and coincidence to bring you whatever it is you seek.

As you practise, you will notice that you are developing a very definite rhythm as you pronounce the numbers. This same rhythm should be used as you use the chant.

You are now ready to begin.

After darkness has fallen, enter your witching circle and light a single white candle. Put out all lights except the candle and awaken your magic power.

Chant the Magic Word, *Misabu*, over and

over again for at least five minutes. Ideally, the chant should begin as a shout and gradually fade away to a whisper.

Pronounce the 'I' as 'ee' and the 'U' as 'oo'.

If there is any likelihood that anyone will hear you, just say the chant in your mind.

I would suggest you begin the chant on a Sunday, at or at least near the Full Moon.

What Will Happen After Casting Your Spells?

Not a lot. There will be no sudden puffs of green smoke, rolls of thunder, or flashes of lightning. Neither will an unclean spirit appear dressed in a scarlet coat, yellow vest, and pale green breeches, with a head resembling a dog, the ears of an ass, two horns and the legs and hoofs of a calf. Nor anything else that the old Grimoires would have us believe are necessary when magic is being worked.

Spells work on the minds of other people. They influence chance and coincidence to attract the outcome that is right for you by harnessing the magical forces around, and within, you.

Chapter 5

ANCIENT SECRETS OF THE CABALA

It is said that God created the world by pronouncing the *Tetragrammaton* correctly and it is regarded as the ultimate Magic Word of Power. The *Tetragrammaton* is an essential part of the Cabala, a form of mysticism that evolved from Judaism. It is the four letter name of God (Yod, He, Vau, He) and is normally pronounced *Jehovah* or *Yahweh* and sometimes *Adonai*.

Please do not try to understand it now, you will not be able to until you have mastered the *Middle Pillar Ritual* revealed in this chapter. But once you are ready for it, I think you will find it to be one of the most profound and rewarding experiences in your life.

Here, too, are the Secret Names of God that magical adepts have used for centuries to invoke the hidden powers of the Cabala, and a most powerful Ritual that will send any unfriendly spirits back where they came from in short order, never to return.

One tradition surrounding the Cabala is that Magic Spells and Rituals based upon its system possess extremely potent effects over all forms of matter. Such magical formulae are naturally much sought after and books containing them are hard to come by.

The Tree of Life

The Cabala is the secret teaching of the ancient Hebrews, concerning the inner meaning to the simplistic doctrines and philosophy of the Old Testament. It forms the basis of modern occult thought. It is immensely complex, taking many years of earnest study and practice to master the merest fraction of it.

The central symbol in Cabalism is the Tree of Life, giving the path to perfection. The idea is that you follow a complex path of spiritual enlightenment up the tree passing through each *Sepher* (divine emanation) until you achieve union with God in *Kether* the Crown.

An interesting aspect of the Cabala is that the achieving of knowledge is likened to sexual union with *Shekinah*, a female personification of wisdom. This is similar to the Gnostic *Sophia*, wisdom given a female personification, only with a much stronger sexual connection as she was a prostitute.

Gnosticism was the main competitor to Christianity in ancient Rome. The Gnostics believed that the Christian *Jehovah* was not the real God but an evil creator of an evil world.

The Power of the Spheres

Sit or lie down, whichever you find most comfortable, at the centre of your witching circle.

If you choose to lie down, use a rug or blanket as a mattress.

Now, begin to breathe rhythmically until the rhythm is established. While inhaling and exhaling in this rhythmic pattern pretend that a sparkling, sphere of light is hovering just above your scalp.

This is the Sphere of Spirit.

See it as clearly as you can.

Speak the First Sacred Name of Power: *Eheieh.*

Repeat three times.

You will feel a tingling sensation in your hands and feet.

Next, form the mental image of a small shaft of white light moving out from the lower half of the sphere of light. The shaft moves down through your head until it reaches your throat, at which you imagine a second sphere of light.

This is the Sphere of Air.

See it as clearly as you can.

Speak the Second Sacred Name of Power: *Jehovah Elohim.*

Repeat three times.

You will experience a sensation of warmth in your throat.

With these two spheres firmly established, pretend that the shaft of light moves slowly down through your chest. Visualise a third sphere on a level with your heart.

This is the Sphere of Fire.

See it as clearly as you can.

Speak the Third Sacred Name of Power: *Jehovah Eloah Ve Daas.*

Repeat three times.

You will feel a vibration throughout your chest cavity.

Now you should imagine the shaft of light moving down through your body to your genitals. At this point you should visualise a fourth sphere.

This is the Sphere of Water.

See it as clearly as you can.

Speak the Fourth Sacred Name of Power: *Shadai El Chai*.

Repeat three times.

You will experience a pleasant sensation in your pelvic region.

Complete this part of the Ritual by extending the shaft of white light to your feet, where a fifth sphere is visualised.

This is the Sphere of Earth.

See it as clearly as you can.

Speak the Fifth Sacred Name of Power: *Adonai Elohim*.

Repeat three times.

The image you have in your mind's eye

should be a shaft of fiery white light running from your head to your toes, inside your body, studded with five gigantic, brilliant white gems – three along the centre and one at each end.

You will now experience the Power of the Spheres physically. A great calmness will surge through your mind, and your skin will prickle with a vibrant current of raw magical power.

It remains only to circulate it and then direct it to change circumstances and situations to your benefit.

The Sacred Names of Power

The Names used in the first part of the Ritual are ancient Hebrew Names of God that have a Mystic Power of their own. They are a true invocation to the hidden occult power of the Cabala, and powerful adepts have used them for centuries. By saying the Names, you are attuning yourself with the power of those adepts, and the still greater powers of the Cabala.

The correct phonetic pronunciations of those names are as follows:

The First Sacred Name of Power is pronounced: *Eh-he-yeh*.

The Second Sacred Name of Power is pronounced: *Yeh-ho-vo El-oh-heem*.

The Third Sacred Name of Power is pronounced: *Yeh-ho-vo El-oh-ah Vay-dah-ass*.

The Fourth Sacred Name of Power is pronounced: *Shad-ay El-kay*.

The Fifth Sacred Name of Power is pronounced: *Ah-doh-nay El-oh-heem*.

Practise each Name a few times until you can say it clearly, firmly and decisively. You are using the raw Magic Power of Higher Spiritual Forces to shape your future.

The Middle Pillar Ritual

Breathe deeply and bring your attention to the Sphere of Spirit above your head. As you exhale slowly, pretend that a liquid stream of white light is beginning to emerge from the sphere and flow down the left side of your body, bathing your left shoulder, arm, hip, leg and foot with its mystic glow.

Try to feel this light being absorbed through the pores of your skin as it flows down the side of your head, and on down your body.

When the stream of light reaches the Sphere of Earth at your feet, begin to inhale slowly and pretend that the stream of light is moving up the right side of your body, back to the Sphere of Spirit.

On the way up it bathes your right leg, hip, arm and shoulder with white brilliance, just as it did to your left side on the way down.

Repeat this imaginary circulation process, down on the left side, and up on the right, until it becomes a fluid movement of imaginary light.

Now add a second flow to the first. This time pretend that the light is moving down the front of your body as you exhale, bathing your face, chest, stomach, thighs, legs and feet in sparkling white light.

Then, as you inhale, imagine the light flowing under your feet and up at the back of your body, flooding white light over your calves, buttocks, back, shoulders and neck.

Repeat this second flow, the down and up motion, until it becomes a fluid movement of imaginary light.

The whole of the Ritual described so far is known as *The Middle Pillar Ritual*. This has taken far longer to spell out in detail than it does to perform. As you finish imagining the circulation of the white light, you can proceed directly to the magic working.

Using the Middle Pillar Ritual to Bring Money

Are you short of money? You can use the Middle Pillar Ritual to bring you what you need in the way of ready cash. Money is associated with the Sun and, to bring it to you, the Sun's magical colour of gold needs to be used.

Perform the whole of the Middle Pillar Ritual. In your imagination, you are bathed in light. Pretend that the white light around you has turned to bright, sparkling gold.

See the golden light as clearly as you can. Try to actually breathe in this mystic light through the pores of your skin. Imagine it circulating within you.

At this stage, only one more step is needed.

Pretend that the money is already flowing into your life. See the money as clearly as you can. Picture it in your possession.

Get involved with the money, love the money, touch and feel it. It is real.

Be confident, as confident as you would be if the money were actually in your pocket or purse.

In theory, it is possible to produce the desired effect at a single attempt. In practice it will be necessary to repeat the process. Decide on a convenient time to perform this Ritual and perform it every day until the money arrives for you to see, feel, touch and possess.

The Ultimate Protection

When we tread the ancient path toward releasing our magic power, it is possible to attract unfriendly spirits to us.

Late one evening, Derek K. was in his study preparing for an exam and chatting with friends online, when something evil came to visit. The lights in the room started flickering, the temperature dropped, and he felt the presence of something unseen in the room with him.

He panicked, and could feel the invisible entity begin to drawn near to him. Very quickly he left the room thinking, 'This can't be happening'.

Upon entering the anteroom, he saw a semi-transparent being looking directly at him. It began to move forward and, as it did so, the lights began to flicker and eventually went out.

By now Derek was scared out of his wits. He went back into his study and located an incantation given to him by a friend.

He read the incantation repeatedly, but could still feel the entity getting closer and closer. Then suddenly, it was gone.

Not surprisingly, the whole weird experience left Derek feeling completely drained and exhausted.

To make absolutely certain that this doesn't happen to you, here is a powerful Cabalistic Ritual that will send any unfriendly spirits back where they came from in short order, never to return.

The Cabalistic Cross

Stand at the centre of your witching circle, with your feet together. Face East. Close your eyes. Pretend that a ball of white light is hovering just above your scalp. With your left hand at your side, raise your right hand above your head, to touch this sphere with your first and second fingers. Keep those two fingers together, and curl your thumb and your third and fourth fingers into the palm of your hand.

Bring your right hand down to touch your forehead, at the same time imagining a shaft of light being drawn down into your body.

Speak the First Magic Word of Power: *Ateh.*

The Word of Power is pronounced Ah-tay.

Without altering the posture of your fingers, bring your hand and arm straight down in front of your chest and touch your breast, imagining the shaft of light extending through your body to your feet.

Speak the Second Magic Word of Power: *Malkuth.*

The Word of Power is pronounced Mal-coot.

Lift your right arm, bending it at the elbow, and point your two fingers at your right shoulder, at which you form the mental image of another sphere of power.

Speak the Third Magic Word of Power: *Ve Geburah.*

The Word of Power is pronounced Vay-gay-voo-ray.

Move your right hand across your body to touch your left shoulder, imagining a second shaft of light passing through your body.

Speak the Fourth Magic Word of Power: *Ve Gedulah*.

The Word of Power is pronounced Vay-gay-doo-lah.

Clasp both hands in front of your chest.

Speak the Fifth Magic Word of Power *Le Olahim. Amen.*

The Words of Power are pronounced Lay-oh-lahm-Amen.

This completes the Ritual and you can rest easy that nothing evil can come anywhere near you, and that all is good and positive around you.

The Flaming Pentagram

Perform the whole of the Cabalistic Cross Ritual. With your left hand at your side, stretch out your right hand with the first and second fingers extended, to draw the sign of the Elder Gods (a pentagram) in the air before you.

Keep those two fingers together, and curl your thumb and your third and fourth fingers into the palm of your hand.

Draw the pentagram, starting with your hand in the region of your left hip and sweeping smoothly upwards to the natural top limit. Imagine the lines of the pentagram as white fire. When the pentagram is complete, draw back your hand and stab it through the middle with your outstretched fingers.

Speak the Sacred Name of Power: *Yod He Vau He.*

The Sacred Name is pronounced Yod-heh-vav-heh.

With your arm outstretched, walk to the South, tracing a line of fire as you go.

Draw a second pentagram and stab it.

Speak the Sacred Name of Power: *Adonai.*

The Sacred Name is pronounced Ah-doh-nay.

Walk to the West, tracing a line of fire as you go.

Draw a third pentagram and stab it.

Speak the Sacred Name of Power: *Ehyeh.*

The Sacred Name is pronounced Eh-he-yeh.

Walk to the North, tracing a line of fire as you go.

Draw a fourth pentagram and stab it.

Speak the Sacred Name of Power: *Agla.*

The Sacred Name is pronounced Ah-ge-lah.

Return to the East, closing the imaginary circle of fire in the centre of the first pentagram.

Extend your arms to form a Cross.

Form the mental image of the archangel Raphael in front of you. See him in yellow robes and imagine air currents flowing from him towards you.

Say *'Before me, Raphael'.*

Form the mental image of the archangel Gabriel behind you in the West. His robes are blue and he stands against a background of the sea.

Say *'Behind me, Gabriel'.*

Form the mental image of the archangel

Michael in the South. His robes are red and he stands against a fiery, volcanic landscape.

Say *'On my right hand, Michael'.*

Form the mental image of the archangel Uriel in the North. He wears dark robes (olive, russet, citrine and black) and stands against a background of fertile earth.

Say *'On my left hand, Uriel'.*

Hold all the images firmly in your mind. Say: *'About me flame the pentagrams. Behind me shines the six rayed star'.*

Repeat the Cabalistic Cross.

This completes the Ritual, which is still secretly practised today as an opening ceremony in many occult Lodges. After you have practised this a few times, and found the swing of it, you will find it equally effective if you merely imagine you are making the gestures.

Chapter 6

THE POWER OF THE MYSTERIES

Spirits, of whom there are millions, reside in what is known as the Astral World, an invisible sphere of existence that duplicates the physical world we live in. It is with the inhabitants of this unseen world that mediums make their contacts at séances.

Until now, access to this unseen world was only possible with astral travel. This is the phenomenon of consciously projecting your 'astral body' from its physical counterpart. The astral body is an exact duplicate of the physical body. It regularly leaves the body during sleep, although there is no memory or sensation of this when you awake. To consciously leave the physical body requires practice and understanding of basic occult laws.

There are many, many books on the market explaining the 'how to' of astral travel but, if you have ever tried any of the many varied techniques to induce astral travel, you will know that it's a very hard thing to do. In fact, for most of us it just doesn't work at all.

That is all about to change.

I will teach you a new kind of astral travel, a simple method that will allow you to 'see' the invisible world around you. You can master it in just a few attempts and, once you do, the astral world will shimmer into view and take shape around you.

If you have done any research into the techniques used up to now to induce astral travel, you will recognise that this occult formula is as different from ordinary astral travel as chalk is from cheese.

The Golden Light

Enter your witching circle. Awaken your magic power. Close your eyes and let your body relax. Once you have done this, let your mind go blank. Think of the inside of your head as being filled with a dense black mist. Now imagine a tiny point of golden light right in the centre of your head.

This Inner Light is your Magic Power given substance through imagination. Let it slowly grow until it fills the entire inside of your head. Hold it that size for a few seconds... then let it grow again until it fills the room. Simply imagine this golden energy field is filling the room, and it will do so.

Now is the time to probe the secrets of the astral world around you. Let your golden energy field begin to feed images of the unseen world into your mind. They will be very faint at first, and it will take a great deal of effort just to become aware of them.

But you will be surprised at how fast this talent develops. One or two attempts should give you a unique occult experience.

When you have thoroughly mastered the ability to probe the unseen spheres around you, you are ready to go further.

Lie down at the centre of your witching circle. Close your eyes and concentrate on the radiant energy of your magical power. Imagine its golden light filling the room. Focus your thoughts on going deeper and deeper into the astral worlds. It is here, at the deeper levels, that you will encounter the truly bizarre inhabitants of this magical dimension.

What will appear before you? That I leave for you to find out, but I can tell you it will be a world far stranger than you can imagine, filled with swirling energies, psychic forces and strange creatures resembling the creations of imaginative movie script writers.

How to Recognise Signs and Omens

Spirits communicate with us through dreams, visions and omens, and can see the future with their unseeing eyes. There are Spirits in the room with you. Does that surprise you? It shouldn't. Spirits surround us twenty-four hours a day.

You need to become aware of the unseen forces that cluster around you. Feel them standing there in silence watching you, sensing your every thought and desire. Once you do, you will not only never be lonely again, but you will also be able to get help to bring your desires to you. Spirits respond to those who respond to them. Only to the uninitiated do things happen by chance.

Have you ever had an advance warning that something was about to happen in your life and then, later that day, found that you had an unusually good or unusually bad experience?

Although you may not have been aware of it at the time, you received an omen – a direct message from the invisible inhabitants of the Astral World.

There is a way that you can spot these signs and omens and know what they mean. The signs and omens most people receive are simple everyday occurrences, but the act of noticing them is what makes them significant.

The signs and omens that are noticed have a definite relation to the character of the events yet to come. The key here is you – what *your* normal reaction is. No one can tell you if anything you see is pleasant or unpleasant.

Only you can decide.

What this means to you is simply this: if you notice something out of the ordinary – a strange bird, a peculiar looking cloud, a door that suddenly jams, odd actions of a family pet, be prepared. Something unusual, either very good or very bad, is going to happen to you in the near future.

A Vision of Gold

During the second half of 1981, I conducted a series of occult experiments with arcane symbols to receive visions and omens, and I can think of no better example of visions experienced by a student of the occult arts than that of Barry M., a Polish psychic who, on 2 October 1981 at 1:40 pm in the afternoon, placed himself into a harmonic state of mind to receive psychic visions of the future. A future that held the promise of easing the financial hardship he was experiencing at the time.

Earlier that day, I'd entertained Barry at my apartment. I had met him through a newspaper advertisement offering home-based psychic development classes, and found him to be quite a character. He was not your typical psychic. He drove an old, beat-up Volkswagen Beetle (in which he would occasionally sleep) and wore the same faded brown leather jacket wherever he went. I regret not knowing him longer.

Over a cup of coffee, the discussion turned to his problems. I bombarded him with questions and, in self-defense I suspect, he agreed to the experiment.

The time was now 1.35pm and, as an aid to his concentration, I darkened the room.

Barry's body became totally relaxed and his breathing deepened. He described the visions as he experienced them, speaking slowly and carefully. His visions were vivid, and he was fully conscious of his physical environment. Barry would occasionally pause; these moments are indicated by three periods (...) in the text.

Almost instantly he began to describe a small circular object moving through the time-field. The visions continued:

'It has got a little chute underneath. It's now producing a sort of shovel, yet not a shovel but a telescopic-like thing coming out from the bottom of it similar to a u-junction.

'It appears like water coming out of it in drops, or it could even be coins...I'm not sure. I'm watching it. It's red in colour. It's dripping into some pool, something liquid.

'Whatever it's going into, it's a ring of sorts. It is dripping something like candle wax and it sets. Possibly melted gold, I don't know. I'm trying to make sense of it.

'Now the u-pipe is being drawn back into this little gadget and there is a yellow light coming through, as if shining on this thing it's spilt out. I see it change into a pair of hands. There seems to be a growth, or change of paper notes of some sort. Paper. A lot of paper in this pair of hands in this yellow light.

'I'm getting a lot of mumbo jumbo. I'm trying to sift through it.

'A door opened and there's a hell of a lot of multiple, glittering colours in this doorway. I am at the moment seeing what appears to be a volcano, or a dead volcano, surrounded by clouds. And a sort of cavity in the centre of this mountain peak. Still looking for the key back here.

'The volcano has not erupted, but sprang a leak, and something is pouring out of it and running down the side of the mountain. I'm following it through the clouds. That's odd, I'm seeing a helicopter at the moment.

'All I'm seeing are hands, at the moment. A lot of hands, as if a lot of people are trying to get a piece of this action.'

Barry began to rub his hand back and forth across his forehead.

'Across my forehead here,' he continued, 'I feel a pressure. Has my face changed?'

I told him that I could see a strange kind of psychic energy, similar to heat waves generated by asphalt highways, rising up from the floor in front of him.

'I see what appears to be a knight on a horse bringing me something. That's what you saw.'

I had earlier in the day experienced a vision of my own, of a knight on horseback.

'Someone just tipped a vase, or a container, and pieces of eight, gold coins spread everywhere.'

Barry began to rub the thumb and forefinger of his right hand together. I asked him why he was doing that.

'I'm feeling the coins, they're real. The vase would have been about two feet tall. I'm going to do something I've not done before. I'm going to put the coins back in the vase and I'm going to bring it back done here.

'I am at the moment seeing a hole in the floor and right directly below it is Earth. I'm going to drop the money through there… and I'm going to hold on to it as it comes down.

'I'm in a paddock. The money is here. I'm trying to find it. I'm looking around. There are mountains in the… in the distance. Not too far away from mountains... or the… ah… I don't know… the Springwood Hills. The feeling here is Elizabeth Drive. On the back roads of Liverpool… no, Rooty Hill, there used to be an army barracks. The only thing I'm getting, an army barracks.'

By 2.30pm the visions had ceased.

As Barry slowly opened his eyes to the familiar surroundings of the living room, he knew he'd had a unique psychic experience. Now we had to decide what it all meant – particularly what the vase was that had held the gold coins.

As far as we knew, it could all have been the wildest fantasy, though it seemed unlikely. The visions had been too clear, too vivid. As we talked into the late afternoon, Barry suggested that a trip to the Elizabeth Drive area would either confirm or deny the validity of the visions.

I agreed.

We both felt a mixture of excitement and anticipation as we drove along the main road leading to the area seen in the visions. Leaving the densely populated areas behind us, it was if we had driven into a rural landscape. Ahead the road disappeared into the horizon and to either side cows grazed peacefully in paddocks dotted with vegetable gardens and solitary houses.

'Look,' said Barry, pointing to a tin can on the opposite side of the road. 'That's what I saw. I'm sure of it.'

I glanced out the window as we pulled over to the side of the road. I was not so sure. The container Barry had seen in his visions was at least two feet tall, and filled to the brim with gold coins, so if this was the right place, the visions had been more symbolic in nature than specific.

I watched Barry walk across the road towards the old tin can. He picked it up, looked inside and threw it back down to the ground. I remained silent as he got back into the car.

'That's what I saw,' he said emphatically.

I nodded.

We sat quietly, watching the occasional car

speed past. Barry was confused. The psychic impression, fascinating as it was, was false. Or so it seemed. He found it difficult to believe that, after all these years, his psychic powers were beginning to fail him.

A truck rumbled past, its raucous noise shattering the oppressive silence of the car, and a thought drifted into my mind. What if the visions represented an event in the immediate future, and not in the here and now?

Barry was the first to speak.

'Let's go,' he said. 'There's nothing for us here, nothing at all.' As we drove back to my apartment, we arranged to meet again the following Tuesday. That would give the money three days to arrive and enough time to prove that the visions weren't totally worthless.

Barry arrived on the appointed day and at the appointed hour, and I wasted no time in asking if he had succeeded in locating the money source. He smiled and told me how, on the Saturday following the visions, he had received $300 from various people for instruction in the occult sciences. The visions had been vindicated.

I never saw Barry again after that day, but I'll always remember our strange adventure together in every detail.

I experienced an omen of my own that day, though I was unaware of it at the time.

As we were driving to the designated area,

we passed a block of flats. Two years later, I would move to that very same block of flats.

Dreamland of the Gods

Streaks of lightning flashed across the night sky as an angry cloudbank gathered over the city. The streets of the city were deserted. The tall buildings that were its heart and soul were dark, unoccupied, forlorn. Into the surrealistic landscape there came a stranger in a land where strangers often met.

He looked up at the sky and waited.

After a long moment a light appeared somewhere deep within the cloudbank. It grew steadily brighter until a strange cigar-shaped object suddenly burst into view. It sat there, hovering silently, emitting blinding rays of intense white light. Suddenly the mysterious craft disappeared back into the cloud.

Minutes passed. Then the clouds parted and revealed a dark, football-shaped object with a row of red lights across its centre. The flashes of lightning behind it added an eerie effect.

It, too, hovered silently for a few moments before rising silently up into the darkness.

I forced myself awake and wrote down as many details of the dream as I could remember.

Readers with a knowledge of UFO incidents may be interested to know that the second object resembled exactly the UFO that abducted police patrolman Herbert Schirmer on 3 December 1967 at Ashland, Nebraska, USA.

The Coming of the Saucers

UFOs first came to the public's attention on 24 June 1947, when Kenneth Arnold sighted nine boomerang-shaped objects flying in formation near Mount Rainier in the Cascade Mountains of Washington State, USA.

Arnold was not the first person to encounter strange objects in the sky. On 21 June 1947, Harold Dahl was out piloting a boat on Pugent Sound near Maury Island, just off Tacoma, Washington. With him were his teenage son, two crewmen and a pet dog.

Dahl glanced up and saw five doughnut-shaped objects circling around a sixth one, at a height of approximately 2,000 feet. The objects were metallic, approximately 100 feet wide with a 25-feet-wide hole in the centre. It had portholes around the perimeter and a near-black observation window on the underside.

Suddenly there was the sound of an explosion and the UFO, around which the other five were circling, showered the area with silver and aluminum flakes. This was followed by a discharging of hot slag-like material which crushed into the boat, killing the dog and injuring Dahl's son on the arm. After this, the five remaining UFOs disappeared from sight.

The Volcano Monster

Those preceding paragraphs may have given you the impression that flying saucers were the only mysterious visitors during those long ago days. Wrong: monsters were also walking the land.

Indians living near the extinct volcano Popoentepell (near Mexico City) said they saw a 100-foot-long snake-like monster with a luminous head making its way to the top of the volcano.

Two Indian wood gatherers were the first to report seeing the monster just after nightfall. They said the monster's head had a dim blue glow with red flashing eyes, and that claws on its feet made foot-deep impressions in the hard soil.

One Indian hermit living on the side of the mountain claimed to have seen the monster off and on for over a year, but had never been bothered by it (*El Paso Herald-Post*, 27 November 1945).

The Secret Power of Dreams

To the people of the ancient world, dreams were signs sent from the gods. They foretold future events and were a source of fascination for both layman and philosopher alike.

Maybe so, but there is another side to these

nocturnal visions. One which has the wherewithal to move all our lives down a very different path.

Dreams are as old as man himself. Always fascinating, sometimes frightening, they reflect the unknown dimensions of the inner mind and can put us in contact with forces far greater than ourselves.

Occultists believe that dreams are the links of connection between the physical and the astral worlds.

Spirits occasionally communicate with us through dreams in order to pass on secret knowledge.

For example, to give power to your desires, imagine tiny, gold-coloured translucent spheres in the air around you, as you hold the desire firmly in your mind.

In dreams, the mind becomes passive and receptive to external influence. Little wonder, then, that other, more advanced, intelligences would choose dream manipulation as a means of communication.

On the subject of dreams, a friend once told me a theory that dreams were the true reality, and the everyday world was just a dream. After I had stopped laughing I told him whoever had come up with that idea must have been very unhappy with his life.

However, now to the details of how to open your mind to alien contact.

UFO Dreaming

An hour before bedtime, sit down with a book about alien abductions and/or UFOs. Try to absorb the essence of the encounters - the kind of clothes the aliens wore, what they did to the abductees, how they communicated, what their main agenda was, how their spacecraft operated. It's helpful to sensitise your mind in this way, although not entirely essential, since time, distance and space are disintegrated within seconds in the dream state. Still, a little preparation can make things easier for you.

Just before you go to sleep, concentrate on a field of golden light, imagining your head to be filled with its radiant energy. UFO Dreaming is a continuation of the Golden Light Ritual.

Hold the golden light firmly in your mind as you doze off. The image of this light must be absolutely clear and vivid in every way. Concentrate on the aliens you are trying to reach. Your sensitised mind will take care of the rest.

Keep a pad and pencil next to your bed and write down as much as you can remember as soon as you wake up.

This is very important, because all of the details of your contact with alien minds will vanish in a few minutes after you arise.

A word of apology: success is not always guaranteed the first time. Persist until a result comes. If you put a great deal of time and effort into making it work, you will have a very unique psychic experience.

Chapter 7

THE ESOTERIC ARTS

This chapter is one of the most mystical in this book of wonders. You will learn how to use a Mystic Power Meditation to transform your life, to make it what you want it to be. You will also discover a simple method to solve your life problems through Spirit Contact. Here, too, is the secret of how to hear a silent voice that knows the future and is ready to reveal its secrets to you.

Mystic Mind Power

Meditation is very much a part of occult practice and is particularly dominant in Eastern philosophy. The purpose of meditation is to focus your thoughts on the unknown dimensions of the human soul. Meditation is by and large a journey into the deeper levels of the human psyche, and this is what makes the study and practice of meditation so interesting.

There are several books on the market explaining the 'how to' of occult meditations, but you can get quick results by taking the following steps.

Inside The Temple

This simple, yet powerful, meditation is designed to set the mystic vibrations going your way. You need no complicated preparations, just carry out the simple instructions as given to change your life in whatever way you wish.

After darkness has fallen, sit alone in a room and light a single white candle. If you wish you can burn a stick of incense. Close your eyes and take a few deep breaths to help you relax.

Now imagine you are seated at the centre of an ancient stone temple, high atop a mountain peak. See the temple around you as clearly as possible. The mental process which you are utilising is called daydreaming, and is a natural function of the human mind.

See in your mind the night sky above. It will be dark and then it will begin to fill with streaks of lightning. Imagine the lightning striking the ground around you. Continue to daydream in this way until the air around you literally crackles with Mystic Power and Force.

It is at this moment that you must focus your complete attention on what it is you wish to achieve.

Allow no other thoughts to enter your mind. Concentrate completely on your desire and how the meditation will help you to achieve it.

Repeat the Mystic Power Meditation daily until you draw your desire to you.

How to Make a Spirit Communication Device

Here is the secret of spirit contact. You'll see how to build a spirit communication device for pennies, and use it to get fast, precise help to solve your life problems. Spirit contact is perfectly safe and you will never come to any harm using these arcane methods of communicating with the Spirit World.

When you are in contact with the Spirit World and when precise information is desired, you can turn to a *scrying* device. This device is a Spirit Communicator (pendulum), and consists of any small object tied to one end of a piece of string.

It is easy to set up a code of communication with any spirit by means of this device.

Many stores that deal in occult supplies will sell you a pendulum, consisting of a small clear plastic ball on the end of a chain. Making such a device for your own use is a simple procedure, and you will get far better results if you make your own Spirit Communicator.

It is a valid magical tradition that the tools that you make with your own hands are the ones that will bring the best results. All you need to do is to tie a piece of string about twelve inches long to a favourite ring or a button that you have worn many times, and your Spirit Communicator is then made. You are now ready to begin.

Between the Living and the Dead

Sit at a table, rest your elbow comfortably and hold the string of your Spirit Communicator between your thumb and first finger, allowing your hand to hang limply from the wrist. Use the hand that you normally write with.

Adjust the length of the string until the weight of the device is an inch or so above the centre of the table. Be sure to work on a firm table, because an unsteady one may contribute a motion of its own and deceive you into misinterpreting the information you receive. When everything is set, hold your hands still until the pendulum has stopped swinging.

Then, speak these words aloud, firmly and decisively:

'Let the dead rise and come to me'.

Make no conscious attempt from now on to make the Spirit Communicator swing, nor should you grit your teeth and defy it to swing. Sometimes two or three minutes will pass before the device begins to move.

In a few moments, the Spirit Communicator should begin to swing in a line of its own accord, indicating the presence of a communicating entity. If it does not respond put it away and try again later, when you are more relaxed.

Some people wonder how anything so simple as this can work. These are the people who have never tried it. Some, however, try it and do not get results. Usually their inbuilt skepticism, doubt or tension foils their effort. But when these conditions are absent, success is almost always instant and automatic.

Getting Answers From Your Spirit Communicator

Once you receive a positive answer, you can proceed to set up an actual code of communication. To do so, hold the Spirit Communicator perfectly still, and say:

'Will this spirit please select a motion of the pendulum that is to mean "Yes".' The Spirit Communicator should move in one of four directions. Follow the same procedure for 'No', 'I don't know', and 'I don't want to answer that question'.

There are only four directions in which the pendulum can move: back and forth, from side to side, clockwise, or anti-clockwise.

At this point, you may ask the spirit any question you desire.

Ask only one question at a time and each time wait for an answer. Needless to say, it should be phrased for a simple 'Yes' or 'No' answer.

Ask it questions to which you do not know

the answer. Check the answers later and judge the validity of the communicating entity from how well it has responded to you.

These early contacts between you and the spirit force are important. Keep your first contact with the spirit world fairly brief. Your obsession with it can be the real danger.

Advanced Spirit Communication Work

Once you are expert at receiving 'Yes' and 'No' answers, you can proceed to a more precise method that will spell out specific answers to your questions. Arrange the twenty-six letters of the alphabet in a semicircle on your usual scrying table, and the words 'Yes' and 'No', as on a Ouija board.

The Ouija board was very popular in the twenties, and many people made their own Ouija boards simply by writing all the letters of the alphabet across a flat surface, and under this all the numbers from zero to nine. They also wrote the words 'Yes' and 'No', as on a real Ouija board. Any smooth object that could slide around was used to spell out messages, such as a wineglass.

Now, by holding the Spirit Communicator over the chart, you can divine precise answers to your questions.

If you succeed in contacting the same spirit a number of times, the spirit will become *familiar*, sense your needs, take instruction readily, and help to bring you what you seek.

The best time to call Spirits from the Inner Planes is on the night of the Full Moon between midnight and 1am.

How to Ensure the Communicating Entity Will Not Lead You Astray

Occasionally you may suspect that some spirit of malicious intent is controlling your Spirit Communicator because the answers seem to be gibberish. At such a time it is well to carry out the Cabalistic Cross Ritual as described in Chapter 5. Then ask that a new spirit step forward. Ask it questions to which you do not know the answer. Check the answers later and judge the validity of the communicating entity from how well it has responded to you.

Creating Your Spirit Contact Book

Once the line of communication is opened, things are going to happen so fast and so often that it will be difficult to keep track of them by mere memory alone.

The easiest way to remember all the practical expressions of your mystical workings is to keep a small notebook in which you write your spirit contact experiences. Call this notebook your Spirit Contact Book. A small pocket diary is ideal, although you may wish to purchase something more ornate for this, your first spirit contact tool.

This is the time to be specific, and your notebook is a handy reminder that contact with a certain spirit will produce a certain result. You will get your first inkling of the Power you are in touch with as you see the miraculous happenings in your life recorded in your notebook.

How Dice Foretell the Future

Dreams, intuitions and hunches, visions and thoughts that will be sent to you from the depths of the Invisible World during your Spells and Rituals will show you the future with great accuracy. However, at times, you will doubt the impressions of your mind.

Until you are perfectly sure and confident of the messages the invisible inhabitants of the next dimension send to you, you can employ a powerful occult tool that will give visible evidence of the future, and reveal its secrets to you.

The esoteric arts offer many unique tools that can be used to get in touch with the future, but none is more accurate than the secret code of communication concealed within the spots of a dice.

Each set of spots has a hidden meaning. Its

secret code reveals events that will soon appear in your future. It is interesting to note that the spots are arranged so that the opposite faces always total the Magic Number Seven (1+6, 2+5 and 3+4). If you multiply the three sevens (7x3 = 21), plus the added value of all the spots (1-6 = 21) plus one for the dice itself we get the following total: 2+1+2+1+1 = 7, the number of days in a week.

Also, the four faces equate to the four seasons and cardinal directions, so in this way dice can be used at any time of the year (seasons) to foretell what is coming (direction) within the next seven days.

The Ritual of Vassago

You need three dice to foretell the future. The three dice can be purchased from any toy store. The material that they are constructed of makes no difference in fortune telling power. To charge your dice with prophetic power, take them into your personal witching circle on a day when you are feeling particularly good.

Place the dice upon a small table at the centre of your circle and begin stirring them clockwise with your right hand for approximately three minutes.

The remainder of the ritual is very important, and it is absolutely essential that it be followed exactly in the manner that I will reveal to you.

After the dice have been stirred thoroughly, pick up one of the dice with your right hand, and speak these words:

'I invoke thee, Vassago, Guardian of the Mysteries, to hear and accept this offering. I hold in my hand the instrument through which thy power, virtue and authority shall manifest. It will forever reveal the truth of what shall come to pass in future times. So mote it be.'

Recite this invocation with each dice, placing them in a neat stack on your left. When the ritual has been completed, your dice are ready to spell out exactly what the future holds in their unique, prophetic code.

Your dice need no special care, but they should be used for foretelling the future only. They should never be used for the playing of any board game if they are to be used for occult purposes.

How to Use Dice to Foretell the Future

Three…a very happy surprise.
Four…an unpleasant letter will be received.
Five…a new friendship will be formed.
Six…a friend will ask a favour of you.
Seven…a new romance.
Eight…a gift of clothing will be received.
Nine…a gambling win.
Ten…a legal action in which you will become involved.

Eleven...a journey to a place of entertainment.

Twelve...a large sum of money will be received.

Thirteen...a period of unhappiness.

Fourteen...a new love.

Fifteen...a warning of approaching troubles.

Sixteen...a sudden, pleasant journey.

Seventeen...involvement with persons at, or from, a distance.

Eighteen...a great rise in life.

On average, the predicted events will come to pass within seven days of the dice being cast. Some, however, will occur almost instantaneously, while others may take a little longer.

It rarely happens but if, at some time in the future, you feel the prophetic power of the dice is slipping, just work the *Ritual of Vassago* to build the mystical power back into your dice.

Note: If you have ever had psychiatric treatment for delusions or any other hallucinatory tendencies, I advise you not to experiment with Spirit Contact: not because of any danger, but simply because the results will be unreliable for you.

Chapter 8

SEX MAGIC TODAY

Modern day witches make loud noises about how straight-laced their ceremonies are, but witches from all times and all places have always recognised the enormous level of magical power contained in the sex act. The idea behind the wide and traditional uses of sex in witchcraft is that at the moment of sexual climax you release a power that can be tapped for magical ends.

The practice of sex magic is widespread. Generally, it is performed along the following lines.

The flickering light of candles illuminates the room. The air is heavy with sweet smelling, constantly burning incense. Red and black drapes hang from the walls and an altar to the demons of lasciviousness and sensuality is placed toward the North.

Its chief ornament is a well-oiled artificial phallus of marble or wood, tall black candles and a chalice. Beside it is a small whip. If the ceremony is an all-night affair, sensuous music is played to heighten the atmosphere.

The Coven Master wears a red robe and the

others wear black cloaks to cover their nakedness, their faces hidden behind small black 'domino' masks.

As the ceremony begins, the coven renounces all other religions, vows to serve the dark forces, and pledges to keep its activities secret.

Sexual offerings are made to the dark spirits attracted to the ceremony. The coven remove their masks and cloaks, and turn their attention to the gratification of the senses. Each member is encouraged to indulge in his or her own perversions to ensure the excitement reaches a fever pitch.

When the Coven Master considers the orgy of wickedness is reaching a climax of excitement, he begins to work the magic, harnessing the sexual energy liberated by the lowering of inhibitions.

Once the initial ceremony is completed, a 'Queen of the Night' (usually a recently initiated member of the coven) is elected to satisfy the sexual demands of the Coven Master.

She is carried to the altar, laid down and surrounded by black candles, and 'worshipped' by the more virile men of the coven. She is stroked, kissed and otherwise stimulated until her passions are aroused. Only then is she brought before the Coven Master who copulates with her, until he is exhausted.

The Mark of the Beast

Aleister Crowley, an infamous black magician of the 1920s, was dubbed by the *Daily Express* as 'The wickedest man who ever lived' and came to believe that he was the biblical 'beast' of the Revelations.

He was, for a short time, a member of the Hermetic Order of the Golden Dawn, but his true interests lie in the OTO (*Ordo Templis Orientis*), a Germanic Magical Fraternity involved in sexual magic.

He took this and adapted it into a new religion, *Thelema*. This was a magical system dedicated to the enlightenment of one's soul via sex rituals held in honor of Pan, the god of earthly existence and often portrayed as the carnal side of man's nature.

In 1920, Crowley established his 'Abbey of Thelema' on a small island off the coast of Sicily, the walls of which were covered with an incredible collection of Crowley's artistic expertise. Frescoes and paintings depicting every conceivable form of sexual deviation adorned the walls.

The Temple of the Abbey (the central hall) contained an altar at the centre of a magic circle, a throne upon which Crowley would sit during the rituals dedicated to magic and sexuality, and various other occult paraphernalia such as an artificial phallus and a whip.

From time to time, Crowley would nominate a willing female disciple to be his idea of the 'Scarlet Woman', a particularly wanton prostitute. He would then subject her to every form of humiliation and degradation his fertile mind could come up with – including branding between the breasts!

After his death at Hastings, England in 1947, his erotic poem *Hymn to Pan* was recited during the funeral services by his few remaining disciples, and an occult ceremony held at his grave. The 'beast' had fallen.

Thank You Letter #5

'Thank you for your letter and advice. Anyway, I've tried your *Asmodeus Spell* with amazing results, also the *Seduction Spell* worked first time and it worked well. The girl in question I had not seen for 18 months. It's a long story, but I could not believe my luck.

'I thought a couple of years ago I would never score with her, and for that alone I thank you. I hope the dark forces continue to give you more Spells, because it's these that seem to work best.

'Once again, I just wanted to thank you for your Spells.'

Signed: C.L., England.

The Demon of Lust

The Clavis Magica Artium describes Asmodeus as a demon of sensuality and luxury. He is also well versed in the sexy art of occult ribaldry, i.e. how to cause a young girl, however prudent she may be, to become maddened and inflamed with lust.

Here is an arcane truth: more people have been seduced and influenced by the occult without their knowledge than by any amount of good looks, wealth, or intelligence.

On the night of the New Moon, enter your witching circle and cover a small table with black cloth (this table might be called your secret altar). Stand a red candle in the centre.

Light the candle.

Awaken your magic power. Gaze into the candle flame, and visualise yourself surrounded by admiring members of the opposite sex.

As you visualise in this way, chant Asmodeus' name over and over again. Ideally, the chant will begin as a whisper and gradually rise until a shout.

When you have ended the chant, extinguish the candle and, in a clear and distinct voice, affirm: *'So mote it be'.*

Now sit back and wait for the opposite sex to come to you.

This is pure black magic. If you have a particular person in mind, try to obtain something that has been in contact with the person you wish to seduce. A hair or a fingernail clipping is best, and hold the item in your hand as you cast the Spell.

Thank You Letter #6

'First of all I decided on the Sex Spell because I needed a woman purely for sex to fulfill my frustrations. I tried the *'Asmodeus Seduction Spell'* as I feel shy, and within a week a lady telephoned me who I had only known for three hours, whom I met six weeks ago.

'She got into my car and she asked for a kiss. After a drink she wanted me to make love to her, which she asked me, and I didn't have to say or do a thing.

'I could not believe that this could happen and no way was she the type who slept around.

'A week later I tried the Spell on a person whom I wanted so much to have sex with. I placed a photograph of the person within the circle and thought deeply of this person and within three days this woman came to visit me. She was explaining that the other night she kept on having sexy dreams leaving her very frustrated, and within a short time we made love.

'I never had to put myself forward in any way, and yet I have always wanted sex with this woman but, being married at the time, I didn't want to be unfaithful to my wife.

'I hope you are convinced that your Spells do work as you must know that they do, because it would be a billion to one chance for this to happen without Spells. I am 37 years of age and this has never happened before in my life, so I am convinced that your Spells do bring us what we seek in life.'

Signed: R.G., England.

The Occult Seduction Spell

For this Spell to work most efficiently you need to obtain a photo of the person you wish to seduce. If you are unable to obtain a picture, draw a sketch of him or her on paper. It doesn't matter whether or not you're artistic: only you are going to see the sketch, and you are aware of what the picture is meant to represent.

To further identify the sketch, write the name of the person under your drawing of him or her.

On the night of the New Moon, enter your witching circle and cover a small table with black cloth. Stand a red candle in the centre and place the photo of the person whom you wish to seduce in front of the candle. Awaken your magic power. Light the candle and say:

'Light the flame, bright the fire.
Red is the colour of desire.'

Put yourself in a highly sensuous mood and gaze into the candle flame. Visualise the person whom you wish to spellbind standing alone in a darkened void. See it as clearly as you can. Now recite the following:

'Powers of night and lustful delight
Go to him/her in the still of night.'

As you speak the words, picture a bright red light slowly beginning to envelop him or her, gradually encircling and enclosing the entire body.

Repeat the conjuration until you have said it three times in all, then let the image fade from your mind.

You will, of course, have been using the appropriate pronoun where the Spell says 'her' or 'him'.

Repeat this Spell each New Moon until results are obtained.

You will note the use of the colour red for these two Spells. Red is the traditional colour used by witches in sexual matters.

Thank You Letter #7

'I tried your *Occult Seduction Spell* on a woman I had a lust for, and who never seemed to have any interest in me, and your Spell worked very well. And one thing that I would like you to know is that when I had your Spell in September 1986, she was my next door neighbour.

'I did your Spell on Friday and Saturday night, and when I did your Spell next morning I strove to be in the presence of the woman concerned so that she could see me. She even begged me to let her come with me to my place. And we had sex for five months. I took every opportunity to touch and fondle her!'

Signed: D. B., Seychelles.

A Magical Threesome

The Grimorum Verum, an eighteenth-century French Grimoire based on the *Key of Solomon*, tells how to cause the appearance of three spirits in your room after supper.

After three days of celibacy, you must clean and tidy your room before breakfast. You leave the room undisturbed all day. There must be nothing left hanging, nor must there be anything left crosswise. Then, after supper, go there secretly, light a good fire, put a white cloth on the table and set three places, with a chair, a roll, and a glass of water at each. Put a chair and a settee beside the bed and, when you retire to bed, recite the conjuration.

When the three spirits appear, they will draw lots as to which keeps you company, and the other two will sit at the table beside the fire. The chosen spirit will sit by the bed and talk to you, answering questions on any subject you care to ask about, and telling you where to find hidden treasure if there is any in the locality. Before departing at midnight, he or she will give you a ring that will assure you of success in love and luck at cards.

What makes this ancient Spell so interesting is the conjuration, for I have discovered that it acts as a kind of secret code of communication between us and the *incubi* and *succubi* – sexual spirits that visit us by night to tempt us with all manner of lusts and depravities. Repeating the conjuration will cause you to have intercourse with them within the reality of an erotic dream.

This Spell works best if it is first worked three days before the New Moon, before retiring to bed for the night, repeat the following conjuration three times:

Besticitum consolato veni ad me'vertat.
Creon, Creon, Creon, cantor
laudem omni potentis, et non-commentor.
Stat superior carta bient
laudem, omviestra principem da montem et inimicos meos o
prostantis vobis et mihi dantes que passium fieri sincisibus.

Repeat the Spell on the following two nights. On average the dreams will occur within three days of working the Spell. Whilst this Spell is designed to bring on erotic dreams, I know of at least one case where an actual physical manifestation occurred.

Thank You Letter #8

'About the incubus: After I did the conjuration I must have dozed off, when a touch on my face woke me up. My night-light was still on and so in this dim light I saw him.

'I guess he was able to search in my mind because he looked quite like my personal prince charming, the answer to a dream come true. He had dark hair, with eyes like burning coals and dark tanned skin.

'There were no words spoken, there was only passion and it was great. I wasn't afraid when I awoke, just curious what will happen.'

Signed: M. S., Germany.

Sex Magic for Couples

If you are happy with the one you love, and there is no need to use Sex Magic to attract a lover or arouse passion in another, then you can harness the tremendous magic power generated in your sexual activity as a means of gaining power in the material word.

Who does not want a better life? And what better and more pleasant way of acquiring it than by that most powerful of all magic – Sex.

Sex, together with a definite thought or desire, is a mighty thing indeed, hence the wide and traditional use of sex in magic for thousands of years. Witches and Occultists from all times and all places have always recognised the enormous level of magic power contained in the sex act.

In the Ritual that follows you can make the irresistible combination of sex and magic work real wonders for you.

First, you and your partner must decide on what it is you seek. Then enter your witching circle and place a pillow, for the female's head, in line with one of the four cardinal points. The direction you choose will depend on what it is you seek.

Once you know your intention you should check with the list in Chapter 3 to know which Elemental Force to invoke.

Now indulge in the sex act, but keep your mind at all times on your magical intention.

That's all there is to it.

Magical Aphrodisiacs

Another tradition of sexual magic and practice is the custom of feeding your partner with certain foods imbued with aphrodisiac properties that will arouse his or her passions.

Aphrodisiac foods are ruled by the stars. They exert a more potent effect if the correct foods are served to the person whose astrological sun sign agrees with the foods concerned.

Thus, by compliance with the Laws of Astrology, a witch can gain better results from his or her actions.

Here is a list of the most suitable aphrodisiac foods for the various astrological signs:

Aries: Cinnamon, pepper and chestnuts. *Taurus:* Grapes and sage. *Gemini*: Carrots and fennel. *Cancer:* Garlic and peppermint. *Leo:* Almonds and celery seed. *Virgo:* Apples and thyme. *Libra*: pumpkin seeds and other nuts. *Scorpio:* Ginger, mustard and onions. *Sagittarius:* Sesame seed and nutmeg. *Capricorn:* Dates and wintergreen. *Aquarius:* Bananas and rye. *Pisces:* Mint and oranges.

The word *aphrodisiac* is derived from Aphrodite, the Love Goddess of the Ancient Greeks whom the Romans called Venus. Of all the goddesses of ancient Greece and Rome, none was more widely venerated than the goddess of love. Every god (even Zeus himself) wanted the beautiful, golden Aphrodite as his wife, but she was too proud and rejected them all.

Chapter 9

THE LAND UNKNOWN

The ancient Grimoires engaged in long and complicated descriptions of the spirit entities that one could conjure with the help of magical formulae, and to which of the planets they were aligned and what powers were attributed to them from the planet. For example, *The Fourth Book of Cornelius Agrippa,* an occult document of dubious origin, has this to say about the forms of spirits in their manifestations:

The Spirits of Saturn appear tall and lean with an angry countenance, having four faces, of which one is in the usual position, another at the back of the head, and two, with beaks, on either side. They also have a face on each knee, of a shining black colour. Their motion is like that of the wind, and it is accompanied with a kind of earthquake. Their sign is white earth. Their forms are a bearded king riding on a dragon; an old bearded man; an old woman leaning on a staff; a boy; a dragon; an owl; a black garment; a hook or sickle; a juniper tree.

The Spirits of Jupiter appear with a sanguine and choleric body; they are of middle stature; their motion is 'horrible and fearful', but they are mild of countenance and gentle in speech. Their motion is that of flashing lightning, and withal thunderous; their sign is the apparition of men about the circle who seem to be devoured by lions. Their particular forms are a king with drawn sword riding on a lion; a mitred personage in a long vestment; a maid crowned with laurel and adorned by flowers; a bull; a stag; a peacock; an azure garment; a sword; a box tree.

The Spirits of Mars have a tall body and choleric, a filthy countenance, brown, swarthy or red in colour; they have horns like the hart, claws like a griffin and they bellow like wild bulls. They have the motion of burning fire, and their sign is thunder and lightning about the circle. Their particular forms are an armed king riding on a wolf; an armed man; a woman holding a buckler on her thigh; a she-goat; a horse; a stag; a red garment; wool.

The Spirits of the Sun appear large of body and limb, sanguine, gross, and of a gold colour tinctured with blood. Their motion is that of lightning; their sign is to produce sweat in the operator. Their particular forms are a king riding on a lion; a crowned king; a queen with a sceptre; a bird; a lion; a cock; a golden garment; a sceptre; tailed.

The Spirits of Venus have a body of medium height and a pleasant visage, of which the upper part is golden and the lower white or green. Their motion is like that of a brilliant star. Their sign is the semblance of maids sporting about the circle and luring the Magician to join them. Their particular forms are a king riding on a camel; a naked maid; a she-goat; a camel; a dove; a white or green garment; the herb savine.

The Spirits of Mercury appear commonly with a

body of middle stature, cold, liquid, moist. They are withal fair, affable in speech, of human shape and like unto armed knights. Their motion is that of silver coloured clouds. Their sign is to cause horror and fear in the operator. Their special shapes are a king riding on a bear; a comely youth; a woman holding a distaff; a dog; a she-bear; a magpie; a garment of many changing colours; a rod; and a little staff.

The Spirits of the Moon have a large, soft, phlegmatic body, even as a dark cloud in colour. Their countenance is swollen, their head bald, their eyes are red and rheumy, their teeth like those of a wild boar. Their motion is like that of a great tempest sweeping the sea. Their sign is a heavy shower of rain about the circle. Their particular shapes are a king like an archer riding on a doe; a little boy; a huntress with bow and arrows; a cow; a small doe; a goose; a green or silver-coloured garment; an arrow; a many-footed creature.

Either the ancient Magi had a wild imagination, or they were witness to some truly bizarre manifestations of supernatural phenomenon. Whatever the truth about these ancient teachings, the belief that such manifestations are possible through the application of magical rites and ceremonies has become so deeply rooted in the occult psyche that it has been endorsed by occultists through the passing of time as being in conformity with occult and arcane laws.

Your Occult Legacy From the Past

There are ancient occult forces for good or evil. To summon these forces and to receive the help the Invisible World can give, it is necessary to make contact.

You are about to enter the world of powerful ancient magic, and the results will amaze you. The Spirits described in this chapter are ancient and possess a power stronger than the centuries. Power to call forth any condition or situation you desire. All this is here for you, in simplified form. You are on the threshold of working genuine magic for yourself to bring you what you seek.

You will find the Secret Names of twenty different Spirits on the following pages. One essential occult belief is that if you know the real name of a Spirit you have control over it. Pronounce the Names exactly as I have written them. If you stumble over a Name the first few times, don't worry, but practise it until you can say it clearly.

Treat these Names with care. Keep them secret from people who do not know about the Magic Power of the Occult.

The word *spirit*, which is derived from the Latin *spiritus*, refers to any disembodied entity, devil, demon or angel. It can be invoked, coerced or otherwise called forth by the magician through the application of those things which are harmonious with it and reflect certain parts of its nature.

The difference between those Spirits willing to help you and those that won't is invariably fear. If spirit invocation is to work, you must do it without any mental reservations.

As you begin to use this Power in your daily life, it will seem as if you are dreaming a strange dream. Answering a call to enter the Netherworld.

How You Can Make Contact With Ancient Occult Forces

Before you cast your Spell, choose the Spirit most suited to what you seek, and write down your wish so that the intent is clear in your mind. You may also wish to time your spell casting with the lunar cycle.

Darken the room in which the Magic is to be worked by drawing the curtains, but have some light coming in. You may choose to burn a single black candle, inscribed with the Name and Power of the Spirit. Loosen any tight clothing and remove any footwear that you may be wearing.

Sit and relax your body in a comfortable chair with your back supported. If you are using your witching circle, position the chair at its centre and face North. Take the phone off the hook to avoid any sudden interruption, and switch off the television.

You are now ready to begin.

Close your eyes for a few minutes and think only of your desire, and how the Spell will help you to receive it.

You are now ready to begin the conjuration.

Once you have thanked the Spirit for its presence, you will need to see through and past the everyday world. Do not peer anxiously, let the stare become vacant.

You will then experience a feeling of a 'clearing mist' followed by a feeling akin to excitement as the Ancient Spirit makes its presence known to you.

The Spirit has no power to harm or influence you. The Spirit can not influence you to do anything you would not do of your own free will.

At this point, take a mind journey and show the Spirit in pictures what must be accomplished. You may also use words and gestures if you wish. You must get involved.

Once the intention has been completed, thank the Spirit for its help and bid it farewell. Very quickly, leave the room, closing the door behind you. Do not enter the room for three hours, as your ability to stay outside is proof that you are in control.

Spell to Pass Exams

Name of Spirit: Alloces.

At any hour of the day from sunrise till noon, thank Alloces for all his help to others in days gone by.

Thank him also for being with you on this day and at this hour, and ask for his kindness and favour at this time. Be prepared beforehand to describe the exam and its details and what you will gain from it.

Spell for Magical Success

Name of Spirit: Amdusias.

At any hour of the day from sunrise till noon, thank Amdusias for all his help to others in days gone by.

Thank him also for being with you on this day and at this hour, and ask for his kindness and favour at this time. Amdusias will sense your needs, take instruction readily, and help to bring your wishes into the here and now.

Spell to Bring Harmony

Name of Spirit: Amon.

Between the hours of 3pm and 9pm and from 9pm to sunrise, thank Amon for all his help to others in days gone by.

Thank him also for being with you on this day and at this hour, and ask for his kindness and favour at this time.

Amon will produce harmony between people

who are at odds with each other, and settle disputes between friends.

Spell to Confuse Enemies

Name of Spirit: Andras.

Between the hours of 3pm and 9pm, and from 9pm to sunrise, thank Andras for all his help to others in days gone by.

Thank him also for being with you on this day and at this hour, and ask for his kindness and favour at this time.

Andras will cause confusion among your enemies. You should be able to name your enemies, and be sure they are the cause of your problems.

Spell to Find Lost Objects

Name of Spirit: Andromalius.

At any hour of the day, thank Andromalius for all his help to others in days gone by.

Thank him also for being with you on this day and at this hour, and ask for his kindness and favour at this time.

Describe the missing item clearly, then sit in a darkened room and pay attention to your stream of thoughts. Act on the information received.

Spell to Bring Money

Name of Spirit: Astaroth.

At any hour of the day or night, thank Astaroth for all his help to others in days gone by.

Thank him also for being with you on this day and at this hour, and ask for his kindness and favour at this time.

Astaroth has proven himself extremely adept at bringing moderate amounts of money to settle existing debts. Be prepared beforehand to describe clearly what bills need paying or what you want the money for.

Spell to Stop Gossip

Name of Spirit: Balam.

At any hour of the day from 9am to noon and from 3pm to sunset, thank Balam for all his help to others in days gone by.

Thank him also for being with you on this day and at this hour, and ask for his kindness and favour at this time.

If you have people who are making your life uncomfortable through gossip, Balam will turn their attention away from you.

This Spell is particularly effective against lies, spite and slander.

Spell to Travel Safely

Name of Spirit: Bathin.

At any hour of the day from sunrise to noon, thank Bathin for all his help to others in days gone by.

Thank him also for being with you on this day and at this hour, and ask for his kindness and favour at this time.

For quick protection, say (or think) Bathin's Name three times.

Spell to Attract the Opposite Sex

Name of Spirit: Beleth.

At any hour of the day from 9am to noon and from 3pm to sunset, cover a small table with black cloth.

Stand a red candle in the centre.

Place a small mirror in front of the candle.

Light the candle and thank Beleth for all his help to others in days gone by.

Thank him also for being with you on this day and at this hour, and ask for his kindness and favour at this time.

Then, look into your own eyes in the mirror. Be relaxed, and blink when you need to. Continue to look into your own eyes for at least two minutes. Then extinguish the candle and go about your business as usual.

When you meet someone of the opposite sex

you wish to impress, look between his or her eyes at the bridge of the nose, for a few seconds.

Spell to Win Contests

This Spell has its most superlative effect if you cast it a few days before you intend to buy a lottery ticket or to enter a competition where the prize depends purely on luck.

Name of Spirit: Bune.

At any hour of the day from sunrise to noon, thank Bune for all his help to others in days gone by.

Thank him also for being with you on this day and at this hour, and ask for his kindness and favour at this time.

Be prepared beforehand to describe exactly how you will use the prize to benefit yourself and your family.

The Powers governing luck are extremely fickle. It is possible for others to be using a Spell or Ritual which is more powerful and may possibly cancel your own Magic.

Spell to Achieve Political Ambitions

Name of Spirit: Cimeries.

At any hour from 3pm to 9pm and from 9pm to sunrise, thank Cimeries for all his help to others in days gone by.

Thank him also for being with you on this day and at this hour, and ask for his kindness and favour at this time.

Use this Spell before you make a personal appearance before an audience.

Spell to Bring Riches

Use this Spell to increase your existing assets.

Name of Spirit: Crocell.

At any hour from sunrise to noon, thank Crocell for all his help to others in days gone by.

Thank him also for being with you on this day and at this hour, and ask for his kindness and favour at this time.

Be prepared beforehand to describe exactly why you need the money and what you will use it for.

Does this Spell really work? Just ask me. I once used it to win $1,200 in a lottery.

Shortly after casting the Spell, I was out walking in a local park when I happened to notice a piece of scrap paper on the ground.

I picked it up and saw that it had a series of names and addresses written upon it.

On returning home, I gave numbers to each letter, using the following numerological values:

A=1, B=2, C=3, D=4, E=5, F=6, G=7, H=8, I=9, J=1, K=2, L=3,
M=4, N=5, O=6, P=7, Q=8, R=9, S=1, T=2, U=3, V=4, W=5,
X=6, Y=7, Z=8

When I'd done that, I played the numbers on every lottery ticket I bought. Within one month I won three lottery prizes, including a $1,200 second prize.

Warning: The conjuring of Spirits for material gain should not be taken lightly, or for granted.

Spell to Overcome Opposition

Use this Spell before being confronted by anyone with whom you need to reach agreement or enter any competitive situation.

It will help you to overcome all oppositions in life.

Name of Spirit: Focalor.

At any hour from sunrise to noon, thank Focalor for all his help to others in days gone by.

Thank him also for being with you on this day and at this hour, and ask for his kindness and favour at this time.

Be prepared beforehand to describe exactly who or what you will be battling against and what you will do when you have won.

Spell to Know the Future

Name of Spirit: Furcas.

At any hour from 4pm to sunset, thank Furcas for all his help to others in days gone by.

Thank him also for being with you on this day and at this hour, and ask for his kindness and favour at this time.

Be prepared beforehand to describe exactly why you want this power, and what the first use you will make of it is.

After casting the Spell, listen for and obey all hunches and intuitions which may reach you, and record what information about the future is given to you in your dreams.

Keep a notebook and pencil beside your bed and make a brief note of your dreams as soon as you wake in the morning.

If you wake in the night, think about what you have been dreaming of and make a note about it before you go back to sleep.

Spell for Honours and Fame

Sit down and think about your main goal in life before casting this Spell; it works better when it can be focused on a particular target.

Name of Spirit: Gusion.

At any hour from sunrise to noon, when the Sun is in the astrological sign of Leo, thank

Gusion for all his help to others in days gone by.

Thank him also for being with you on this day and at this hour, and ask for his kindness and favour at this time.

Spell for Protection From Physical Harm

This is another simple piece of Magic that brings powerful protective forces to you.

Name of Spirit: Halphas.

At any hour of the day, thank Halphas for all his help to others in days gone by.

Thank him also for being with you on this day and at this hour, and ask for his kindness and favour at this time.

For quick protection, say (or think) Halphas' name three times.

Spell to Vanquish Enemies

Use this Spell when you know who your enemies are.

Name of Spirit: Haures.

At any hour from sunrise to noon, thank Haures for all his help to others in days gone by.

Thank him also for being with you on this day and at this hour, and ask for his kindness and favour at this time.

Be prepared beforehand to name your

enemies, and to describe exactly what you will do when your enemies are defeated.

Spell to Cause Discord

Use this Spell if people are deliberately harming or opposing you.

Name of Spirit: Leraje.

At any hour from 3pm to 9pm, and from 9pm to sunrise, thank Leraje for all his help to others in days gone by.

Thank him also for being with you on this day and at this hour, and ask for his kindness and favour at this time.

Be prepared beforehand to name those you wish to see disrupted.

This Spell is also useful for breaking up undesirable personal relationships.

Spell to Protect the Home

Name of Spirit: Malphas.

At any hour of the night, thank Malphas for all his help to others in days gone by.

Thank him also for being with you on this day and at this hour, and ask for his kindness, favour and protection at this time.

Malphas will repel burglars, thieves and physical attackers from your home by working on their minds if they try to intrude.

The flat I once shared with my father was

burgled one day. Although the burglar would have had plenty of time to ransack the place (both my father and I were out, and did not return for hours), he stole only some small change and a pocket-watch from one room. He also left behind the crowbar he used to break in. The police were mystified and said: 'Something must have frightened him'.

Spell to Dispel Evil

If you are certain that someone is using black magic or similar sorcery against you, use this Spell.

Name of Spirit: Orobas.

At any hour of the day, thank Orobas for all his help to others in days gone by.

Thank him also for being with you on this day and at this hour, and ask for his kindness and favour at this time.

Orobas will return curses, evil spells and other similar hexes to the person sending them. He or she will then begin to experience unknown fears, anger and faulty judgment.

Spell to Discover Hidden Talents

Name of Spirit: Purson.

At any hour from 9am to noon and from 3pm to sunset, thank Purson for all his help to others in days gone by.

Thank him also for being with you on this day and at this hour, and ask for his kindness and favour at this time.

After casting this Spell, relax in a chair and let your mind flow freely. Listen to any hunches or impulses which come your way to improve your existing skills.

Spell to Bring a Lover

Use this Spell to meet a lover who is exactly suited to your needs, will be delighted with you and will satisfy your every desire.

Name of Spirit: Sallos.

At any hour from sunrise to noon, thank Sallos for all his help to others in days gone by.

Thank him also for being with you on this day and at this hour, and ask for his kindness and favour at this time.

Sallos will bring a lover to you suited to your needs.

Using Ancient Magic to Draw Money to You

The Power of Ancient Magic can be made to work for you in many different ways. If you wish to have money whenever you want or need it, try this. Place an old, unused jar in a place where you pass it and see it several times each day.

Then ask the Spirit Astaroth to help you fill

the jar with money, easily and quickly. You will be amazed at how, each time you pass, you will have an irresistible urge to put into it every piece of loose change you have in your pockets. Almost instantly, it will fill with money: a seemingly endless supply of needed cash.

Thank You Letter #9

'The magic has worked unbelievable miracles for me. It is indeed a true source of occult power. I mostly gain money from the magic, I have been winning lotteries etc. So I just wanted to let you know that I have been having lots of luck thanks to you.'

Signed: G. R., England.

Important Things to Remember

Spells are the fun part of what we call Magic; simple gestures, uttered words, seemingly illogical actions, frowned upon by the scientific Mind, nevertheless make strange and wonderful things happen for the person who casts them. The casting of Spells is based upon the arcane belief that to speak a desire is to cause the desire to be fulfilled.

Whenever a specific area of your life is in need of help, awaken your magic power, and cast whatever Spell is appropriate to your desire. It is the Spell that draws out your power and sends it on its way.

When it comes to spell casting, there's always a chance of first time success if the desire is strong, though it usually does take time and practice to achieve results. The single most important ingredient that makes Spells work is the emotion you invest in them.

The Spells and Rituals in this book must work for you, because they have already worked for other people no different from you.

Now it's your turn.

ADDENDA

Inside the Invisible World

In this book, you've discovered:

1. The cornerstone of witchcraft is the coven. It is lead by a Coven Master.

2. The purpose of the coven is to build magic power amongst its members to achieve the coven's common objectives.

3. Covens hold great feasts on certain nights each year. Special nights on which white witches gather to celebrate their devotion to the moon goddess Diana, and the goat-footed god of fertility, Pan, indulging in drink, laughter, love and song.

4. The more interesting covens indulge in an orgy of wickedness where all the instincts are given free reign.

5. There are various forms of secret initiation ceremonies depending on the type of coven one seeks to join.

6. The initiate is led naked to the centre of a magic circle with her hands tied behind her back, and blindfolded. She then repeats a solemn vow, and is presented to each member of the coven who greet her with a kiss.

7. Contrary to popular belief, not all witches belong to covens. Many work alone and with just as good results using the Magic Power of witchcraft as if they were working with a group. Using this magical power is simplicity itself.

8. The warlock of the Middle Ages, desiring to arouse love and passion, was required to make a figure of wax to represent the woman whose company he desired above all else.

9. White Magic is worked from the first quarter until a Full Moon, and Black Magic from the last quarter until a New Moon.

10. The Knights Templar was a debased Christian sect that practised Occult Rituals.

11. It's a good idea to work a Protection Ritual on a regular basis.

12. The pentagram (five-pointed star) is a tool used by both witches and magicians to keep evil forces at bay. The pentagram represents man - the five points being his head, two arms,

and two legs.

13. In reading these words, you will learn many ancient secrets of the occult.

14. The old Grimoires were hand-written books of Magic Spells, invocations, herbal recipes, incantations and other magical lore.

15. When witches work their Rituals, they work naked.

16. A Ritual to summon the Magic Power within you.

17. Different sensations often accompany the awakening of your Magic Power.

18. Whenever a specific area of your life is in need of help, cast whatever Spell is appropriate to your desire. It is the Spell that draws out your Power and sends it on its way.

19. Spells are the fun part of witchcraft.

20. The casting of Spells is based upon the arcane belief that to speak a desire is to cause the desire to be fulfilled.

21. The secret that makes most Spells work is the emotion you invest in them.

22. An ancient Magic Word used in the Orient, which is said to have remarkable powers.

23. A powerful Money Spell that has proven extremely successful for others, as it will for you.

24. Green is the traditional colour used by witches in money matters. Green is the colour of Mother Nature and is also the colour of paper money; dollar bills are green.

25. A Love Spell that has worked Magic for others, as it will for you.

26. That certain sounds (chants) create unique magical vibrations, the physical manifestation of which is called Magic.

27. Chants should be spoken aloud in a sort of 'up and down' rhythm.

28. Witchcraft draws its power from the Elemental Forces of Earth, Air, Fire and Water, and how to align yourself with these forces.

29. Gnomes are the Elemental Spirits of the earth, and a simple Spell to help you to enlist their aid in your affairs.

30. Modern day witches make loud noises about how straight-laced there ceremonies are, but witches from all times and all places have always recognised the enormous level of magical power contained in the sex act.

31. Sex Magic Rituals and Ceremonies are still secretly practised today.

32. Sexual offerings are made to the Dark Spirits attracted to the ceremonies.

33. The Demon of Lust is summoned on the night of the New Moon.

34. The Occult Seduction Spell is best worked on the night of the New Moon, and requires a photo of the person to be seduced.

35. In witchcraft, red is the traditional colour used by witches in sexual matters.

36. The Conjuration to summon the *incubi* and *succubi* works best if it is first worked three days before the New Moon.

37. Aphrodisiac foods are ruled by the stars and exert a more potent effect if the correct foods are served to the person whose astrological sun sign agrees with the foods concerned.

38. The word 'aphrodisiac' is derived from Aphrodite, the Love Goddess of the Ancient Greeks, whom the Romans called 'Venus'.

39. Sex backed by a definite thought or desire is a powerful magical force.

40. You can make the irresistible combination of sex and Magic work real wonders for you.

41. The Cabala is the secret teaching of the ancient Hebrews, concerning the inner meaning to the simplistic doctrines and philosophy of the Old Testament, and forms the basis of modern occult thought.

42. One tradition surrounding the Cabala is that Magic Spells and Rituals based upon its system possess an extremely potent effect over all forms of matter.

43. Spirits communicate with us through dreams, visions and omens, and can see the future with their unseeing eyes.

44. The signs and omens most people receive are simple everyday occurrences, but the act of noticing them is what makes them significant.

45. The signs and omens that are noticed have a definite relation to the character of the events

to come.

46. Dreams, intuitions and hunches, visions and thoughts that will be sent to you from the depths of the Astral World during your Spells and Rituals will show you the future with great accuracy.

47. The Ritual that will transform dice into genuine occult tools.

48. You need three dice to foretell the future.

49. The three dice should be cast into a circle measuring approximately seven inches in diameter, drawn on a piece of paper.

50. On average, the predicted events will come to pass within seven days of the dice being cast.

51. Meditation can help improve your quality of life.

52. In Spirit Contact, a Spirit Communicator is used to set up an actual code of communication.

53. You may ask the Spirit any question you desire. Ask only one question at a time and each time wait for an answer.

54. Occasionally you may suspect that some spirit of malicious intent is controlling the Spirit Communicator.

55. In advanced Spirit Contact work, you can divine precise answers to your questions.

56. It is best to keep your first contact with the Spirit World brief.

57. The easiest way to remember all the practical expressions of your Spirit Contact experiences is to write them down in a small notebook.

58. You call this notebook your Spirit Contact Book.

59. Powerful Ancient Spirits can bring about any event or condition by unobserved means.

Other Titles

A Prescription from The Love Doctor: How to find Love in 7 Easy Steps - Dr Joanne 'The Love Doctor' Coyle
Burnt: One Man's Inspiring Story of Survival - Ian Colquhoun
Cosmic Ordering Guide - Stephen Richards
Cosmic Ordering Connection - Stephen Richards
Cosmic Ordering: Chakra Clearing - Stephen Richards
Cosmic Ordering: Oracle Healing Cards – Stephen Richards
Cosmic Ordering: Oracle Wish Cards – Stephen Richards & Karen Whitelaw Smith
Cosmic Ordering: Rapid Chakra Clearing – Stephen Richards
Cosmic Ordering: You can be Successful - Stephen Richards
Die Laughing: War Humour from WW1 to Present Day - George Korankye
Life Without Lottie: How I survived my Daughter's Gap Year - Fiona Fridd
Internet Dating King's Diaries: Life, Dating and Love – Clive Worth
Mrs Darley's Moon Mysteries: A Celebration of Moon Lore and Magic – Carole Carlton
Mrs Darley's Pagan Whispers: A Celebration of Pagan Festivals, Sacred Days, Spirituality and Traditions of the Year – Carole Carlton
Past Life Tourism - Barbara Ford-Hammond
Rebel Diet: They Don't Want You To Have It! – Emma James

The Hell of Allegiance: My Living Nightmare of being Gang Raped and Held for Ten days by the British Army – Charmaine Maeer with Stephen Richards
The Real Office: An Uncharacteristic Gesture of Magnanimity by Management Supremo Hilary Wilson-Savage - Hilary Wilson-Savage
The Tumbler: Kassa (Košice) – Auschwitz – Sweden - Israel - Azriel Feuerstein (Holocaust survivor)
Wisdom of the Heart – Flora Rocha